Advanced Lucid Dreaming

The Power of Supplements

How to Induce High Level Lucid Dreams & Out of Body Experiences

Written By Thomas Yuschak
AdvancedLD, Ltd

Published by Lulu Enterprises
ISBN 978-1-4303-0542-2

This book can be purchased at www.AdvancedLD.com
The Author can be contacted at:
tyuschak@AdvancedLD.com

Special Thanks

Thank you to everyone who made publishing this text possible.

Thank you to Scot Stride for taking the time to review this text and for providing so many valuable suggestions.

Thank you to my beautiful wife and to our amazing boys for helping to open my eyes, my mind, and my heart.

May this text help others go where I have been.

Disclaimer

This text summarizes how the author has used a variety of legal, non-prescription supplements to induce high level lucid dreams and out of body experiences. The author suggests that his approach may produce similar results in a wide variety of people of different background and culture. The author strongly recommends however, that any individual, who is interested in attempting an approach that utilizes supplements for the purposes of lucid dream enhancement and/or out of body experiences, consults a qualified physician before adding any supplement or any combination of supplements to his/her diet. The author and AdvancedLD, Ltd (from here on jointly referred to as AdvancedLD) also strongly recommends that any person who purchases or reads this book abide by the following:

1. The supplement approach outlined in this book is intended for adults only. Persons under the age of 18 should not take any supplements for any reason without first consulting with a qualified physician.
2. AdvancedLD shall not be held responsible in anyway for the misuse of the information contained within this book.
3. AdvancedLD strongly recommends that all persons contact his/her physician before starting the program outlined in this book in order to get a doctor's approval prior to taking any supplements discussed in this book.
4. AdvancedLD insists that if the reader has any known or suspected medical conditions, that may include but is not limited to; pregnancy, heart disease, high blood pressure, mental disorder, kidney disorder, liver disorder, immune system disorder, history of stroke, history of seizure, etc, then the reader will contact a physician and get a physician's approval prior to taking any of the supplements discussed in this book.
5. AdvancedLD shall not be held responsible in anyway if dosages beyond those stated are taken by the reader and result in negative effects on health and/or well being.
6. AdvancedLD shall not be held responsible in anyway if the profound effects of lucid dreaming and/or out of body experiences have a negative effect on the reader's psyche and/or mental health. These experiences are extremely profound and therefore the reader must judge for him/herself

or have a professional psychologist judge for him/her whether or not he/she is ready to undergo such an experience.

7. AdvancedLD makes no claims as to what one can accomplish in the lucid (or out of body) state and passes no judgment on the "true" meaning of these experiences.

8. The reader agrees not to forward, publish, or distribute this book or the details held within, in any form or manner.

9. The reader is solely responsible for attaining a physician's approval before taking any supplement discussed in this.

10. The reader assumes all liability if he/she passes this information to others without fully divulging the risks and recommendations set forth in this text.

Table of Contents

Part 4: Improving Your Odds

Foreword:

Conscious dreaming is a fascinating aspect of the human mind. Not until the late 1970's did there emerge a scientific proof that a person could recognize and be aware they were dreaming. Lucid dreaming has come a long way since then and we can thank Green, Tholey, Hearne, LaBerge, Woresly, Garfield, Blackmore and others for their essential contributions. By far the most valued contributions were made by LaBerge who has been active in this field for nearly 30 years.

Many techniques and innovations for lucid dreaming have emerged during this time, benefiting many a person wanting to explore their personal dream environment. Presently, the techniques available to prospective oneironauts (dream explorers) include: State-Testing, Intention, Reflection-Intention, Autosuggestion, MILD (Mnemonic Induction of Lucid Dreams), WBTB (Wake-Back-To-Bed), WILD (Wake Induced Lucid Dreams), CAT (Cycle Adjustment Technique) and others. These mental techniques involve training your mind to become more cognitively aware during dreaming, so you can become lucid. In addition to these entirely mental techniques, electronic techniques, in the form of dream masks, were invented. These included the DreamLight, NovaDreamer and DreamMaker. Electronic devices are intended to cue the dreamer during REM sleep (either optically or auditory), helping them to recognize they are dreaming and become lucid.

Fortunately, there is plenty of room for growth and expansion from new techniques and innovations. My own research into electronic means of helping induce lucid dreams led to the design of a lucid dream induction system (LDIS). This system was my attempt to improve upon the versatility and reliability of a dream mask based on modern electronics, imaging technology and software. After two working prototypes and some very encouraging test results, I can confidently state that a first-rate system is possible, one which can be produced affordably for the dreaming consumer.

So far I've mentioned two avenues available to the oneironaut, the mental and the electronic. Both of these approaches to learning lucid dreaming have found their place in the oneironauts toolbox. However, there is a third and exciting avenue that offers much potential for growth – this is the neurochemistry approach.

Neurochemistry is a branch of neuroscience that involves the study of the chemical processes in the brain. By studying these processes scientists are endeavoring to understand the underlying molecular bases for memory, emotions, cognition, behavior and diseases of the brain like Alzheimer's. Some of the molecules being studied are: Glutamate, Histamine, GABA (Gamma-Amino Butyric Acid), Acetylcholine, Serotonin, Dopamine, Norepinephrine and Nitric oxide. These neurochemicals, and others, are players in a fascinating electro-chemical drama that runs continuously in our brains from conception to death.

The same neurochemicals that play important roles in our waking state are also present in our sleeping state. Neuroscience has led to a clearer understanding of what's happening chemically in the brain during the sleep cycles. Chemicals, like Melatonin, change during the course of a normal sleep period and help manage our circadian rhythms. Other chemicals are also present, in varying amounts, during REM sleep when lucid dreaming mainly occurs. Of these chemicals, the neurotransmitters are the most important, for they carry the electro-chemical signals throughout the brain's neural pathways.

Although there is no scientific study that links specific kinds and quantities of neurotransmitters to lucid dreaming, I surmise a relationship does exist. Many times would-be oneironauts will diligently practice a mental technique, like MILD, or combine it with a dream mask, only to experience discouraging results. Sometimes they try multiple techniques and still struggle. These techniques work superbly well for some and abysmally for others; the only difference may be the levels of certain neurotransmitters during REM sleep. If there were some way to safely boost certain of these neurotransmitters during REM sleep, the success rate may rise, turning frustration into joy.

The headline news is there exists a way to increase these neurotransmitters by ingesting certain dietary supplements. These supplements comprise a lucid dreaming technique which I term Lucid Dreaming Supplements (LDS). LDS are over-the-counter vitamins and supplements that aid in helping the brain attain a neurochemical state which is conducive to having a lucid dream.

Not surprisingly, LaBerge has also done some research into these neurotransmitters and identified a type of supplement that works remarkably well at boosting Acetylcholine (ACh) levels by inhibiting Acetylcholinesterase (an enzyme that breaks down Acetylcholine into choline and acetate). The presence of an AChEI

(Acetylcholinesterase Inhibitor) works by increasing the levels and activation of ACh. Cholinergic neurons are involved in the synthesis of ACh and believed to modulate our level of wakefulness. Taking supplements that effectively raise ACh levels affect the wakefulness of the dreaming brain and hence its ability to become more aware.

LaBerge was able to clinically show that ingesting certain AChEI's does improve the ability to become lucid. His study is just the tip of the iceberg in the LDS technique and underscores the fact that certain supplements favorably improve an oneironauts odds of becoming lucid. Many over-the-counter supplements are available that affect the various neurotransmitters; this makes the LDS technique fairly wide open to experimentation and refinement. I have personally taken some of these supplements and consequently enjoyed some long and memorable lucid dreams.

After corresponding with Thomas Yuschak on his approach to the LDS technique I am very pleased and impressed by his work. He has worked hard to identify specific supplements that, when taken at the right time and in healthy dosages, can open the doors to many oneironaut who need help. Either taken alone, or combined with the existing mental and electronic techniques, in a complementary manner, supplements can reward the oneironaut with a more powerful toolbox.

This book is an important first step in introducing to the oneironaut a new and exciting lucid dreaming technique: a technique that promises to make it easier to consciously dream, and explore an elusive aspect of our inner selves.

Scot L. Stride
Pasadena, California
October, 2006

Introduction:

Why I wrote this book: My main goal in writing this book is simply to share what I have learned through personal experience about the power of non-prescription supplements in achieving high level lucid dream experiences and/or out of body experiences. There is a quiet movement growing among lucid dreamers who have found that certain natural substances provide a catalyst to increased dream memory, vividness, and lucidity. Unfortunately, there is little information available to act as a guide for these individuals. This has led to much speculation, hearsay, and misguided approaches that have resulted in absolutely nothing spectacular. The few who have experienced positive results often find they fade with time and become infrequent at best.

Furthermore there are those who are putting there own health at risk because they do not fully understanding or appreciate the correct approach and the important factors one must consider when utilizing a supplement approach to lucid dreaming. What is missing is a comprehensive guide that removes the guesswork altogether and sets people on the correct path of development. This book is my attempt at such a guide.

It is my sincere belief that lucid dreaming can have a dramatic and positive effect on the global society and culture as a whole, and can help to open our eyes to the potential we all hold inside of us. In order for that to happen however, advanced lucid dreaming must become available to the general public. Typical lucid dreamers struggle with lucid dream frequency, length, recall, vividness and control. The method presented in this book addresses all of these issues and opens the door for almost everyone to experience extremely high level lucid dreams.

At the time of this writing there is no other book available that provides a comprehensive method of using natural, and generally healthy non-prescription supplements as a means of producing extremely high quality and long duration lucid dream experiences. That sets this book apart from all others and will hopefully aid in waking up the general public to the wonders and powers of lucid dreaming.

What this book is and what this book is not:

This book is <u>not</u> a comprehensive list of supplements that have proven to have a positive impact on dreaming and/or lucid dreaming. There are many supplements available which have some effect on how and what we dream and it is not my goal to create a long and relatively useless list. Instead I focus on the supplements that have had the most profound effects on my own dream/lucid dream development and, more importantly, I provide a means of comparing all supplements by the mechanism they use rather than the names they are called. In this way I provide a method of comparing any other supplement that one feels might have the potential to enhance lucid dreaming. Furthermore, I have included sections that discuss the effects of the supplements when taken individually as well as when taken in different combinations.

This book is <u>not</u> an overly technical treatise on the neuroscience of sleep or dreams. Although some basic concepts and definitions are included as a means of providing a better understanding of how supplements can function to increase the quality, frequency, and duration of lucid dreams, I have purposefully tried to keep the science talk to a minimum. It is my goal that the reader can fully understand and take advantage of the insights this book provides.

This book is <u>not</u> an authoritative reference on modern day dream theories; a fascinating topic, but one that is beyond the scope of this text. I will briefly summarize the two major schools of thought however, because they both play a major role in determining which supplements might work best.

This book is <u>not</u> a one size fits all book. What has proven to work excellently for me may not be right for you. Even though I will share my detailed supplement schedule, including exact doses and consumption times, you should consider this as a point of reference only. You will find that in general, I have placed a very high regard for my own personal health and happiness. I expect you to do the same. Blindly following a schedule may cause you harm in the long run, so I have tried to include the knowledge you need to optimize your own supplement program as well as experience first hand the effects of each of the supplements described.

Finally, this book is <u>not</u> a basic lucid dreaming book. I have written it primarily for experienced lucid dreamers who want to take their explorations to a higher level. If you have not yet experienced a lucid dream then I strongly encourage you to put this book down and go buy one of the excellent books aimed at getting you started in this wonderful field. After you have "gone in" and seen for yourself what a lucid dream really is, then come back to this book and take advantage of the methods contained herein. Lucid dreaming is a skill you must develop with practice and moving at the correct speed will get you much further in the long run.

So what IS this book?

This book is my experience and my method of how I have successfully been able to generate high level, long duration lucid dreams on regular basis using a specific combination of legal, over the counter, and generally healthy dietary supplements. This book not only gives the final recipes that work for me personally but also details the means I used to determine these recipes so that anyone can intelligently develop the right combinations for themselves.

Lucid Dreams vs Out of Body Experiences

There is considerable debate about the relationship between lucid dreams and out of body experiences. Some people believe that an out of body experience is a special type of lucid dream. I am one of those people. Two types of lucid dreams are often talked about among enthusiasts: DILDs and WILDs. A DILD (Dream Induced Lucid Dream) is the more prevalent type of lucid dream in which a person is asleep and dreaming when they notice something odd and suddenly realize they are in the midst of a dream. DILDs start as regular non-lucid dreams. A WILD (Wake Induced Lucid Dream) is characterized by moving directly from the awake state into the dream state with no loss of consciousness. One moment you are conscious in your physical body and the next moment you are conscious in your dream body. During the transition from the physical to the dream you can undergo some intense sensations such as a feeling of floating, strong vibrations, and/or rapid accelerations. These are the same sensations that are often referred to in most OBE accounts. Furthermore, when the transition from one body to the other is complete, there is about an 85% chance that you will find yourself standing in your bedroom. At this point you can walk around the house at your leisure. At some point the surroundings transition into a different locale either spontaneously or by conscious effort. This type of WILD is an OBE by all classical definitions and the methods described in this book result in WILDs about 90% of the time. To simplify the writing, I will refer to either lucid dream or WILD with the understanding that the experience is synonymous with OBEs.

What is a high level lucid dream?

The definition of lucid dreaming is, in my opinion, overly simplistic. According to Stephen LaBerge, a popular author and experimenter on the subject, lucid dreaming is defined as "dreaming while knowing that you are dreaming." Those experienced in lucid dreaming understand however, that the quality of the experience can vary greatly from dreamer to dreamer as well as from dream to dream. In the 10 or so years I have been practicing lucid dreaming I continually ranked my experiences by a number of criteria including: duration of the dream, sensory vividness, ability to recall the experience, and the ability to control my reasoning, emotions, and will; all while staying actively involved within the dream. Another important criterion in advanced lucid dreaming is the frequency in which you can enter the lucid state. Here is a comparison of high level lucid dreaming to average lucid dreaming:

Criteria	Average LD	High level LD
Duration	5-10 minutes	Longer than 30 minutes
Frequency	Less than two nights per week	Two or more nights per week
Sensory Vividness	All senses functioning	All senses functioning at a heightened level
Dream Recall	Moderate - May forget details or have fuzzy memory	Excellent – memory is as good as waking events.
Control of Reason	Moderate - May remember some details of physical life while dreaming such as your name but may not remember what your goals for the dream are.	Excellent - Able to recall many details of the physical life while dreaming and are able to stay focused on dream goals.
Control of Emotion	Moderate - may get caught in a feeling of fear if events turn negative.	Excellent - Able to totally let go of fear because of absolute knowledge of the dream state.
Control of Will	Moderate - may be able to fly but may not be able walk through walls or alter the dreamscape around you.	Excellent - Nothing can stop you from what you want to accomplish. Advanced flying possible. Ability to alter the dream to meet your goals.

Using the supplement approach outlined in this book I have 2 to 3 nights per week of high level lucid dreaming. The dreams generally last in excess of an hour and can occasionally last as long as two and half hours. My senses function as well as they do in waking life and my dreams generally include the use of all my senses. I continually show high levels of control that include easy access to my memories from my physical life, total lack of fear even in the most adverse situations, the ability to successfully carry out my dream experiments, and the ability to easily manipulate my dreamscape. This isn't bragging, it's the power that the right combination of supplements can have on lucid dreaming. Furthermore, once one can repeatedly experience high level lucid dreams, they can focus on unlocking the secrets that our contained within.

Although many readers will undoubtedly be drawn to the sections of this book that cover the "best of the best" of the available dream enhancing supplements or the sections that detail my personal and exact method of achieving frequent and consistent, long duration lucid dreams, I recommend reading this book from start to finish. This book has a wealth of information so you may want to revisit the first few chapters after you have finished the complete book. This approach will give you a deeper understanding of the topic and better prepare you to optimize your own personal supplement schedule.

If you are new to lucid dreaming I strongly encourage you to read some of the other wonderful books that describe the basic techniques. My favorites are:

The Lucid Dreamer
A Waking Guide for the Traveler Between Worlds
By Malcolm Godwin (1994)

&

Exploring the World of Lucid Dreaming
By Stephen LaBerge and Howard Rheingold (1990)

I have also included a reference section at the end of this book which contains some very useful links and articles. I encourage you to read as much as possible.

One Final Note

The supplements outlined in this book, enhance lucid dreaming by affecting the levels of specific neurotransmitters in the brain during sleep. These supplements are <u>not</u> hallucinogens and they are <u>not</u> controlled substances. They are available as over the counter dietary supplements and do not induce any type of drug like intoxication if taken while awake. With the exception of Nicotine, they are not addictive and are generally considered to be a healthy addition to your diet. One group is known to increase memory, another group is known to increase focus and attention, a third group is known to increase motivation and creativity, and the last group is known to reduce stress, improve mood and increase quality of sleep.

There are quite a few supplements described in this book. Everyone has a different comfort level when it comes to taking supplements and it is important to understand that it is not necessary to try every combination described here. Start with one or two of the main trigger combinations and build from there.

Part 1:

Theoretical Background

1

Opening Remarks

This section of the book summarizes some important concepts that have been developed in the field of neuroscience. Neuroscience is a field that is overflowing with its own terminology and it is important not to confuse or undermine the topic at hand by including unnecessary definitions or highly technical discussions. That being said, there are some concepts and insights that are absolutely essential to the understanding of how natural supplements can be used to enhance lucid dreaming. Therefore I have tried to keep this section as simple and straight forward as possible yet still include a basic understanding of the topic.

I should also note that I have mixed feelings about the field of neuroscience. On one hand it can not be ignored that the field is expanding our understanding and knowledge about how our brains process data and influence our thoughts and emotions. On the other hand however, it is impossible to hold in high regard a field that is built upon a foundation of destructive experimentation on other living animals. This inefficient and barbaric approach highlights our own ignorance and lack of real understanding as well as fully demonstrates the great strides needed in our own evolution.

Before introducing some of the important terms and concepts associated with the neuroscience of sleep and dreams, we need to briefly review the basic sleep cycle, the REM rebound effect, and the two predominate theories concerning how our brains dream.

A quick review of these topics will help clarify the relevance of the terms and concepts presented.

2

Review of the Sleep Cycle

Our sleep generally moves in cycles, first moving from wakefulness down into a deep, regenerative sleep, then coming back up toward wakefulness, then back down again and so on. Sleepers generally move through four to six of these cycles per night, with each cycle lasting between 70 and 110 minutes.

Each sleep cycle is divided into two distinct phases: non-REM sleep and REM sleep. Furthermore the non-REM sleep phase is sub-divided into four stages that transition us from wakefulness (or REM) into deep sleep and then back up again. The cycles merge and transition from one to another in the smooth continuum we call sleep.

During the deepening stages of non-REM sleep the body becomes increasingly relaxed with brainwaves becoming slow and regular and with blood pressure, temperature and muscle tone all decreasing. REM sleep, on the other hand, is characterized by an increase in heart and respiratory rate, rapid and irregular eye movements, increased blood pressure, as well as paralyzed muscles from the chin down.

The first cycles of the night tend to have shorter REM periods and longer periods of deep sleep. This trend reverses as the night goes on. The later cycles have longer REM periods and shorter deep sleep periods.

By morning, most sleepers spend almost all of their time in stages 1, 2 and REM sleep with very little or no deep sleep (stages 3 and 4). Infants are unique in that they spend approximately 50 percent of their sleep time in REM sleep.

The National Institute of Neurological Disorders and Stroke provides this description of the five sleep stages.

Stage 1 (Drowsiness) – We drift in and out of sleep for about 5 to 10 minutes and can be awakened easily. Our eyes move very slowly and muscle activity slows.

Stage 2 (Light Sleep) – Our eye movements stop and our brain waves (fluctuations of electrical activity that can be measured by electrodes) become slower, with occasional bursts of rapid waves called sleep spindles. Our heart rate slows and body temperature decreases.

Stages 3 and 4 (Deep Sleep) – Slow brain waves called delta waves begin to appear, interspersed with smaller, faster waves. By Stage 4 the brain produces delta waves almost exclusively. It is very difficult to wake someone during stages 3 and 4, which together are called deep sleep. There is no eye movement or muscle activity. People awakened during deep sleep do not adjust immediately and often feel groggy and disoriented for several minutes after they wake up.

REM Sleep – During REM sleep, our breathing becomes more rapid, irregular, and shallow, our eyes jerk rapidly in various directions, and our limb muscles become temporarily paralyzed. Our heart rate increases, our blood pressure rises, and males develop penile erections. People tend to have the most vivid dreams during this stage of sleep.

<u>Neurotransmitters control the sleep cycle</u>: Of particular interest to us is that the brain controls the sleep/wake cycle by releasing various chemicals in the brain called neurotransmitters. These chemicals act on neurons in the brain that essentially "switch on and off" the various stages of sleep and wakefulness. Since sleep and wakefulness are influenced by different neurotransmitter signals in the brain; foods, medicines, and herbs that change the balance of these chemicals affect whether we feel alert or drowsy, how well we sleep, and how much time we spend in the REM phase of sleep as well as how much we dream.

3

Review of the REM Rebound Effect

It is an interesting fact that your body strives to maintain a balanced sleep schedule. It is very difficult to deprive your body of deep sleep or of REM sleep, nor should you want to. Deep sleep is strongly associated with body rejuvenation and is imperative for maintaining proper mental and physical health. It is well known that in times of sickness or injury your sleep schedule will shift to include longer and more frequent periods of deep sleep. The body is healing itself. It is also well known that depriving your body of deep sleep can result in negative effects on both your mental and physical health including a weakened immune system, increased levels of agitation and stress, and a generally lower feeling of well being. As a lucid dream enthusiast you mustn't sacrifice your deep sleep in the pursuit of higher quality lucid dreams. This approach is unsustainable at best. If you deprive your body of deep and restful sleep on one night, in addition to feeling energy deprived on the following day, you will drop into longer periods of deep sleep on the next night in order to make up for the lost time. Any method of lucid dream enhancement must not sacrifice your quantity or quality of deep sleep if it is to be worth anything significant.

There is an interesting counter part to this sleep characteristic. If you suppress REM sleep for a period of time, your body will be strongly encouraged to make up for the lost time spent in this state, and the next time you fall to sleep you may experience an effect referred to as REM rebound. REM rebound can be described as prolonged periods of REM sleep due to prior periods of REM suppression. This effect is commonly seen among alcohol abusers and marijuana smokers. Both alcohol and THC (the active chemical in marijuana) are known to suppress REM sleep. If high enough levels of these substances are in the bloodstream at sleep onset (a common case for the users) REM sleep will be suppressed. If the user decides to clean out their system by discontinuing use, the individual will commonly experience several nights of increased REM time and will commonly experience long and vivid dream experiences. Keep in mind that the most vivid dream experiences (as well as most lucid dreams) occur during REM sleep. Although the REM rebound effect is a somewhat indirect method to increase REM time, it is still a valuable tool that the lucid dream enthusiast has at their disposal.

4

Predominate Dream Theories

The descriptions in this chapter are mainly based on an article titled "DREAMING AND REM SLEEP ARE CONTROLLED BY DIFFERENT BRAIN MECHANISMS" written by Mark Solms, Academic Dept Neurosurgery, St Bartholomew's & Royal London School of Medicine.

There are two predominate theories regarding dreaming. The first theory can be called the REM dream theory, the brainstem dream theory, or perhaps the cholinergic dream theory. The second theory can be called the Forebrain dream theory, the cerebral activation dream theory, or perhaps the dopaminergic dream theory.

The first theory (which I refer to as the cholinergic theory) has been around since the 1950's when the first links between the REM sleep phase and dreaming were discovered. The theory quickly developed the concept that REM sleep is required for dreaming to occur. This belief was based on the fact that 70-95% of normal subjects who were awakened from the REM state report that they have been dreaming whereas only 5-10% of non-REM awakenings produced similar reports. In the mid 1970's it was discovered that REM sleep was essentially controlled by various mechanisms located in the brainstem and this finding resulted in a wide spread belief that these same mechanisms were also responsible for dreaming.

Specifically it was determined that the cholinergic brainstem mechanism could switch on or off the REM sleep phase and therefore dreaming by controlling the release of specific neurotransmitters. According to this theory, REM sleep (and hence dreaming) is switched on by the release of a neurotransmitter called acetylcholine (ACh) and turned off by the release of a different neurotransmitter called serotonin. One could conclude from this theory that the neurotransmitter ACh controls REM and dreaming.

Probably the most disheartening aspect of this theory is that it assumes that cognition plays practically no role in dreaming. The brainstem simply causes a random firing of neurons whose electrical impulses travel to the cognition center of the brain (forebrain) where they are passively synthesized by its memory system into a "best fit" for otherwise incoherent data. In other words the random impulses make it to the forebrain which tries to force meaning to them. It is this process that generates dreams. Although this theory explains the illogical and nonsensical dreams we sometimes experience, it doesn't capture at all the lucid dream experience in which the dreamer directly influences and controls the dream plot and setting. In support of this theory, it has been shown that drugs/herbs that promote the release of ACh within the brainstem can not only generate REM sleep but also generate dreams.

The second theory (which I refer to as the dopaminergic theory) is, in my opinion, more sophisticated, elegant, and complete than the cholinergic theory and is substantiated by a strong clinical basis. The dopaminergic theory tries to fill in the holes left by the cholinergic theory. For example, between 5-30% of REM awakenings do not elicit dream reports and at least 5-10% of non-REM awakenings do elicit dream reports that are indistinguishable from REM dream reports. According to the dopaminergic theory, it is the forebrain that causes dreaming to occur and not the brainstem. This assumption has a number of important consequences. It is well known that the forebrain has little, if any effect on REM sleep. Therefore the conclusion must be that REM sleep is not required for dreaming to occur. One of the clinical facts that provides the basis for this theory is that brain lesions which occur in the forebrain area can totally halt dreaming in an individual without having any affect on REM sleep. It was also noticed that the lesions which halted dreaming were located in the same region of the forebrain targeted in the prefrontal leucotomy (i.e. frontal lobotomy) operations used as a means of behavior control. It has been confirmed that 70-90% of these operations yielded complete or nearly complete loss of dreaming in the subjects. It is this region of the brain that is rich with fibers connecting frontal and limbic structures with dopaminergic cells. This system was the target of the leucotomy because it is believed to control the goal seeking and pleasure seeking mechanisms. Damage along this system produces disorders characterized by reduced interest, reduced initiative, reduced imagination, and the reduced ability to plan ahead. These facts strongly suggest that dreaming is generated by this dopamine circuit. Further evidence supporting this theory is that when L-dopa (a popular drug used to combat Parkinson's disease by increasing the level of dopamine within the brain) is administered to patients in the night time hours, dream frequency and vividness are greatly increased even though there is no corresponding increase in REM sleep. Furthermore, the dopaminergic theory suggests that dreaming is not chaotic in nature but rather manifests from specific and highly complex cognitive processes.

So if REM sleep is not responsible for dreaming, how does the dopaminergic theory address the high correlation between REM sleep and dream reports? This theory suggests that instead of REM sleep being required, a more general state of cerebral activation during sleep is required. REM sleep is often referred to as paradoxical sleep because the brain is both asleep and simultaneously highly activated. The vast majority of dream reports that occur outside of REM sleep are associated with stage 1 or stage 2 sleep (i.e. very light sleep). All of these stages, including REM, line the border between deep regenerative sleep and the waking state.

The fact that dreaming can be artificially generated by the administration of a variety of stimulant drugs, including both cholinergic and dopaminergic agents is open to a similar interpretation. Of crucial theoretical importance is the fact that dopaminergic agents increase the frequency, vivacity and duration of dreaming without similarly affecting the frequency, intensity and duration of REM sleep. This observation, together with the equally important fact that damage to specific areas of the frontal lobe obliterates dreaming but spares the REM cycle, suggests a specific dopaminergic `dream-on' mechanism which is dissociable from the cholinergic `REM-on' mechanism.

So according to the dopaminergic theory, two independent events must occur in order to spawn the dream state: First the subject must undergo cerebral activation during sleep (where REM initiation accounts for one form of such activation) and secondly, the dopaminergic circuits located in the forebrain must also be engaged.

What can the lucid dream enthusiast learn from these two theories?

These two theories provide the basis of the method outlined in this book so it is important to highlight the important findings as they relate to our goal of lucid dream enhancement. The following list is a summary of those findings:

- The release of specific neurotransmitters in the brain control which sleep state we are in as well as activate our internal dreaming mechanism.

- Foods, medicines, and herbs can impact the levels of specific neurotransmitters in the brain.

- Most vivid dream experiences occur during REM sleep but can also occur in stage 1 and stage 2 non-REM sleep.

- The neurotransmitter acetylcholine (ACh) has the ability to switch on and maintain REM sleep.

- The neurotransmitter serotonin has the ability to switch off and suppress REM sleep.

- REM sleep only provides one of the two requirements needed for dreaming to occur.

- The second requirement is that the dopaminergic circuit must be engaged.

- The neurotransmitter dopamine can engage the dopaminergic circuit.

Using the above guidelines one should be able to easily generate long duration vivid dream experiences. But there is still something missing from the equation. What is it that distinguishes regular dreaming from lucid dreaming? Lucid dreaming is a unique state: the body is asleep yet the mind is awake and self-aware. In this state we are neither fully asleep nor are we fully awake, we are simultaneously in both states. I believe this unique state is achieved when the levels of certain neurotransmitters are increased beyond what is typically associated with sleep and more closely resemble levels associated with being awake. Acetylcholine is a key lucidity trigger because, among other things, it increases our wakefulness. Another excellent lucidity trigger is a neurotransmitter called norepinephrine which is mainly associated with being awake rather than with being asleep. It is also for this reason that dopamine, which heavily promotes dreaming, does not necessarily promote lucid dreaming (this is not to undermine the profound effect that dopamine has on lucid dreams) and why serotonin must be used indirectly to aid in lucid dream enhancement.

Before discussing how supplements can be used to adjust the levels of these neurotransmitters, as well as the strategy that we should follow in order to promote high level lucid dreaming, it helps to briefly summarize the role that each of these neurotransmitters (serotonin, acetylcholine, dopamine, and norepinephrine) play in our daily lives.

5

Neurotransmitters and Dreaming

Our brains are similar to a computer in a number of ways. Our senses gather information and input the data into the brain. The brain processes the data, stores it, and produces some type of output. Just like a computer, the brain manages all this by sending millions of tiny electrical impulses back and forth across millions of nerve and chemical pathways. The brain controls and guides these impulses by the release of specific chemicals called neurotransmitters.

A neurotransmitter is a natural chemical in the brain responsible for transmitting messages from one nerve to another. If you were to compare the role of nerves and neurotransmitters to an electrical circuit, the nerves would be represented by the copper wires and the neurotransmitters would be represented by tiny switches that can direct a current to specific groups of wires (nerves). The neurotransmitters are responsible for activating (or de-activating) specific parts of our brain. By doing so, they are responsible for waking us up, putting us to sleep, and making us dream as well as playing a vital role in controlling our state of mind. Our ability to recall the past, our level of alertness, as well as our emotional state are all directly influenced by the levels of specific neurotransmitters within the brain.

There are four primary neurotransmitters that control our waking and sleep cycles. The four primary neurotransmitters are: **Serotonin**, **Dopamine**, **Norepinephrine**, and **Acetylcholine**.

It will become clear in reading the following sections that these neurotransmitters control a delicate balance within your brain and body. In general, everything you eat affects this balance and medicines and herbs can have an amplified affect. Boosting or suppressing any of these systems by excessive amounts will undoubtedly have a negative impact on your life and health. However, small modulations can yield profound benefits. This is the basis of treating most mental diseases like Alzheimer's, ADD, depression, bipolar disorder, Schizophrenia, and many others.

For our purposes it is better to error on the side of conservatism and follow the rule of thumb that "less is better" and that exceeding the effective dosages is pointless.

Serotonin (5-HT): Of the neurotransmitters that we will discuss, serotonin plays the most complex role in our daily lives and probably the most indirect role in lucid dream enhancement. It is the only one of the four that can act as both an excitatory transmitter and an inhibitory transmitter. Serotonin plays a significant role in both wakefulness and sleep. It is involved in the regulation of mood, pain, appetite, and deep regenerative sleep. Serotonin deficiencies have been determined to be a cause for depression, certain types of migraine headaches, bipolar disorder, and anxiety. Also low serotonin levels tend to make it more difficult to focus one's thoughts, may be associated with poor appetite control (obesity), and are a cause for insomnia.

Increased serotonin levels, on the other hand, are associated with decreased depression, decreased anxiety, increased relaxation, increased drowsiness, decreased sex drive, increased non-REM sleep, and suppressed REM sleep. Drugs that increase serotonin levels, like Prozac, can relieve stress and combat depression and are a major focus of ongoing research.

If serotonin levels become too high however, one may experience a phenomenon known as Serotonin Syndrome. This is a serious and potentially life-threatening medical condition characterized by mental confusion, hypomania, agitation, headache, coma, shivering, sweating, fever, hypertension, tachycardia, nausea, diarrhea, muscle twitching, over responsive reflexes, tremor, insomnia, sleep disruption, and unrefreshing sleep. This syndrome is usually caused by combining drugs that each affect the serotonergic system in similar and amplifying ways, such as by combining St. John's Wort (a popular non-prescription herb that can simultaneously boost serotonin, dopamine, and norepinephrine levels) with other serotonin boosting drugs. With this in mind one should always be aware of negative drug interactions that can occur when combining various supplements. Informative decisions and conservatism are a must.

Serotonin and sleep: Serotonin plays an important role in regulating sleep. As we drift off to sleep, serotonin levels begin to rise and continue to do so as we move down into the deepest stages of non-REM sleep. At this point serotonin levels start to decrease as we move from deep sleep back up through the lighter stages and diminish completely when we enter REM sleep. Therefore the amount of serotonin in your system has a direct impact on which stage of sleep you are in. More serotonin generally implies deeper levels of non-REM sleep. For this reason, serotonin boosting drugs are widely used to combat insomnia.

Serotonin and dreams: Foods, medicines, and herbal supplements that increase serotonin levels have repeatedly been shown to cause more vivid dreams. One must ask how this is possible since it appears that increased serotonin levels reduce the time spent in REM sleep (the stage where the most vivid dreams tend to occur). The most common explanation is that serotonin based dreams are caused by the REM rebound effect. Serotonin dreams tend to occur in the morning hours when the medications are wearing off and serotonin levels are dropping. This suggests that during the first half of the night, while these levels are elevated, REM sleep is suppressed and more time is spent in the deeper non-REM sleep stages. As serotonin levels drop, the body compensates for the lack of REM sleep by maintaining lower levels for extended periods of time. This results in longer and more intense periods of REM sleep in the morning hours. Even though the sleep stages have been rearranged a bit (more deep sleep in the first half of the night and more REM sleep in the second half of the night, the net effect is a balanced night's sleep. Furthermore, it has been my experience that supplements that increase serotonin levels tend to generate more calm and relaxing dreams. There is also a marked increase in vividness that is very refreshing. The negative aspect of serotonin dreams is that they seem to be harder to remember than those related to the other neurotransmitters. This highlights an interesting point: vivid sensory experience does not imply vivid memory of that experience.

<u>Serotonin and lucid dreams</u>: Serotonin can affect lucid dreaming in a number of ways; some of which are positive and some of which are negative. On the positive side, serotonin boosting supplements can cause REM rebound which can set up extended periods of REM sleep in the morning hours (or more specifically: after the supplements have mostly worn off). Remember most lucid dreams occur during REM sleep, so longer periods of REM can result in an increased chance of having a lucid dream along with being longer in general. Furthermore, serotonin boosting supplements can increase your quality of sleep. Although this may not be apparent yet, we will see that some of the supplements discussed, significantly increase the time spent in REM sleep. If these supplements are taken too early in the night, it is possible to experience a drastic reduction in deep non-REM sleep. This will result in feeling energy deprived the next day. This feeling can be reduced if these types of supplements are taken after 4 or 5 hours of sleep because a larger percentage of deep sleep occurs during the first half of the night. Furthermore, if these types of supplements are taken after 4 or 5 hours of sleep and if a serotonin boosting supplement is taken just before bedtime, the result can be one of a balanced night's sleep with extended time spent in a high level lucid dream. This is a very important factor to consider when trying to have high level lucid dreams three or more times per week. If your sleep is not balanced on any individual night it will try to rebalance itself on the following night (or nights). If you further deprive yourself of deep non-REM sleep, your body will try even harder to rebalance itself. The result is that you begin to feel more and more energy deprived due to this conflict you're putting your body in. Eventually the body will start to win and your lucid

dreams will suffer in both duration and frequency. Although this is an indirect benefit of serotonin boosting supplements, it is one that needs to be considered and taken advantage of.

The negative characteristic of serotonin boosting supplements is they will significantly decrease your odds of becoming lucid if they are still in your system during a lucid dream attempt. For this reason one must be careful and thoughtful of both the dosages and the consumption times of these types of supplements. Remember that REM sleep is normally associated with increased levels of acetylcholine and reduced levels of serotonin. Because the method described in this book depends on moving directly from wakefulness into REM sleep in order to initiate a lucid dream, it is important that serotonin levels not be too high during the attempt.

Serotonin and supplements: Serotonin taken orally does not pass into the serotonergic pathways of the central nervous system because it does not cross the blood-brain barrier. However, the amino acid Tryptophan and its metabolite 5-hydroxytryptophan (5-HTP), from which serotonin is synthesized, can and do cross the blood-brain barrier. It is believed that 5-HTP is more effective than Tryptophan at increasing levels of serotonin inside the brain because it more readily crosses the blood brain barrier and because it is the direct precursor to serotonin. Another interesting supplement that acts via the serotonergic pathway is Melatonin. Melatonin is the substance in the brain that serotonin is metabolized into: Serotonin → Melatonin. There are some studies that suggest that Melatonin does not suppress REM sleep although I personally doubt this is the case. All three of these substances are available as a dietary supplement and all have been cited as causing vivid dreams. I have not experimented with Tryptophan, but have had good success with both 5-HTP and Melatonin. These substances will be discussed in detail in a later section of this book.

Dopamine: Dopamine is most famous for its stimulant and pleasurable effects, and also appears to play an important role in learning and controlling your body's movement and balance. Dopamine plays a central role in our body's natural reward system and therefore is a crucial factor in motivation.

Due to the generally positive feelings associated with increased levels of dopamine, virtually every drug of abuse, including heroin and other opiates, alcohol, cocaine, amphetamine and nicotine activate the dopamine systems to some degree or another. Elevated dopamine levels tend to make people euphoric, confident, aggressive, and more alert. It has even been suggested that an increase in dopamine levels result in an enhancement in verbal fluency and creativity.

Decreased dopamine levels tend to make people more tired, forgetful, and generally lacking drive and vitality. Lower than average dopamine levels also contribute to low levels of self esteem and libido.

There are a number of psychiatric disorders associated with dopamine imbalances. For example, Schizophrenia is thought to be caused, at least in part, by excessive levels of dopamine and Parkinson's disease has been shown to be related to a significant dopamine deficiency. Mood disorders, including certain types of depression are also thought to be related to dopamine deficiencies within the brain.

Another interesting and important factor is how the aging process takes an inevitable toll on dopaminergic neurons via oxidative stress. Dopamine content of the brain is stable until around age 45, and then decreases linearly by about 13% every decade. When the loss of dopamine reaches around 30% Parkinsonian symptoms may surface. This may also partially explain why people in general, have a stronger lust for life and libido in their younger years than in their elder years.

Dopamine and sleep: Unlike serotonin, dopamine does not seem to play a major role in regulating the sleep cycle in that the dopamine dependent neurons undergo only sight modulations over a twenty-four hour period.

Dopamine and dreams: Some of the most interesting effects on dreaming attributed to dopamine have come from reports of Parkinson's disease patients who take the dopamine increasing drug, L-dopa, as part of their treatment. It has been shown that increasing dopamine levels during sleep can have a dramatic affect on dreaming, making dreams more vivid, longer in duration and perhaps more nightmarish. This is true even though the increased dopamine levels do not have a significant impact on REM sleep. The affect of dopamine on dreams with the corresponding lack of affect on REM sleep has caused a shift in modern day dream theories. No longer do scientists believe that REM is exclusively required or even necessary for dreaming. Although this may be the case, let's not forget that the majority if lucid dreams do seem to occur in REM sleep.

My own experience with dopamine dreams has been extremely interesting. Dopamine dreams tend to be action packed and consistently carry the theme of having to overcome some kind of adversary. Furthermore, dopamine dreams tend to be fully participatory in that you are always actively caught up in the action rather than passively observing it from the sidelines. When describing dopamine dreams they often sound nightmarish (vampires, snakes, gun battles, physical attacks are common dream plots) yet the experience of dopamine dreams is very different from what I consider to be a nightmare. My emotional state during a dopamine dream is one of extreme confidence and totally lacking in fear. Even though there is always an adversary present, the typical theme is one in which I rise up, directly face the adversary, and prevail. When I wake up I tend to feel triumphant, confident, and motivated.

Dopamine and lucid dreams: Dopamine plays an important role in producing high level lucid dreams; however it typically doesn't act as a lucid dream trigger. By this, I mean that increasing dopamine levels in the brain doesn't seem to result in more frequent lucid dream experiences. That being said, increasing dopamine levels result in a profound effect on the ability to control the dream if you do become lucid. The enhanced confidence and lack of fear that was prevalent in the non-lucid dopamine dreams is also present in the lucid dopamine dreams. It is often said that you can do anything in a lucid dream as long as you believe you can. The increased confidence resulting from dopamine gives you the power to believe that you really can do anything. The result is nothing short of miraculous! Consider the example of flying. Most likely every lucid dreamer has taken to the skies at some point or another. But just because you can fly doesn't mean that you can fly well. Many lucid dreamers site poorly controlled and clumsy experiences and a large number of experiences are probably better described as floating rather than really flying. This is not the case when dopamine levels are elevated. High speed, high precision superman style flying becomes the norm rather than the exception. Also consider the case of changing your dream surroundings. The most common approach of accomplishing this is for the lucid dreamer to start spinning with the intention of the surroundings changing to meet their desires. Many lucid dreamers struggle with this. Once again dopamine has a profound effect. Just the spinning alone is incredible and easily outperforms world class ice skaters in speed, acceleration, and duration. Of course the best part is where you wanted to go, you have arrived. These are just two of the countless number of examples of enhanced dream control available via the dopaminergic pathway.

Dopamine and supplements: Dopamine taken orally does not pass into the dopaminergic pathways of the central nervous system because it does not cross the blood-brain barrier. The immediate precursor to dopamine is a chemical called L-dopa and it does pass through the blood brain barrier. There are two types of L-dopa; a purified synthetic form that is available with prescription only, and a natural occurring form that is present in several species of beans. The species that contains by far the highest L-dopa content is called Mucuna Pruriens. This herb is available as a dietary supplement and has been standardized to varying concentrations of L-dopa content. There are other dopamine precursors that are readily available (namely phenylalanine and tyrosine) but Mucuna Pruriens provides the most direct method of increasing dopamine levels. I will discuss Mucuna Pruriens in detail in a later section of this book.

Acetylcholine (ACh): Acetylcholine was the first neurotransmitter to be identified in the early 1900s. ACh plays a major role in the stimulation of muscles, memory, thinking, learning, as well as regulating sleep and controlling emotions. Within the brain, acetylcholine is thought to play a major role in the formation, storage, and recall of memories. Due to this fact, acetylcholine is the focus of an enormous amount of research and is the current basis for the treatment of Alzheimer's disease and dementia. Due to its role in the stimulation of muscles however, acetylcholine has also been targeted by several strong poisons. For example, Curare is a poison that blocks acetylcholine receptors and can cause severe muscle paralysis. On the other side of the spectrum, some types of nerve gas act to prevent the breakdown of acetylcholine and result in severe muscle spasms.

Slightly elevated acetylcholine levels are associated with good memory, ability to learn, and increased time spent in REM sleep. Decreased acetylcholine levels are associated with poor memory (Alzheimer's disease), inability to think clearly, poor reasoning skills, fatigue, and suppressed REM sleep.

Another interesting and important fact is that as we age the levels of acetylcholine present in our brains tend to decrease. This has a negative impact on our ability to remember and even to think clearly. In advanced Alzheimer's disease, where the memory has almost totally stopped functioning, acetylcholine levels can be as much as 90% lower than normal levels. There is a wealth of clinical evidence suggesting that people should supplement their diets with acetylcholine boosting nutrients in order to help ensure a nimble mind and hence a good quality of life during the senior years.

Acetylcholine and sleep: ACh plays a major role in the regulation of sleep. ACh levels start to drop as we drift off to sleep and reach their lowest levels when we are in the deep, non-REM stages of sleep. As we move back up toward REM sleep, ACh levels increase and reach levels compared to the waking state during REM sleep. Acetylcholine and serotonin work together in an inverse relationship in order to control our sleep.

Deep non-REM sleep → High Serotonin + Low Acetylcholine

REM sleep → Low Serotonin + High Acetylcholine

This pairing of acetylcholine and serotonin to produce the different sleep stages has some important implications. To experience the rejuvenation of deep non-REM sleep, it is not sufficient to just boost your serotonin levels but rather it must be coupled with a decrease in acetylcholine levels. To experience the dream rich REM state it is not sufficient to just boost your acetylcholine levels but rather it must be coupled with a decrease in serotonin levels. This subtle point has important implications when it comes to choosing a time to initiate a lucid dream. Since the body tries to enter the deep, non-REM stages during the first part of the night and does so by increasing serotonin levels in the brain, it is best not to try to artificially raise the acetylcholine levels (via a supplement) during this period. Doing so does little to promote lucid dreaming and essentially robs you of the deep sleep you need. So instead of putting your body in conflict with itself, it is by far more effective to let the body rest naturally for 4 or 5 hours before stimulating the cholinergic system with supplements.

Acetylcholine and dreams: Acetylcholine has a profound effect on dreaming and the supplements that boost acetylcholine levels tend to cause long and vivid dream experiences. Acetylcholine plays a dual role in dream enhancement: increased time spent in REM sleep PLUS improved memory of the dream experience. The role in memory is often overlooked when discussing the dream benefits of acetylcholine. It may be even that the memory boost plays the bigger role causing you to simply remember the dream better. Whether it's the memory boost or the REM boost that plays the bigger role in dream enhancement is up for debate, but the fact that increasing ACh levels leads to long and vivid dream experiences can not be denied.

Acetylcholine and lucid dreams: Acetylcholine has a profound effect on lucid dreaming. The supplements that increase ACh levels have the ability to actually trigger lucid dream experiences when used correctly. They do so by allowing you to move directly from the waking state into a vivid dream state without losing consciousness. Recall that there are two kinds of lucid dreams commonly discussed among enthusiasts: DILDs and WILDs. A DILD is characterized by the dreamer already being within a dream before lucidity occurs. In these cases the dreamer usually recognizes something peculiar and then suddenly become aware that they are dreaming. A WILD is characterized by an unbroken continuum of consciousness as the dreamer moves from the conscious state into the dream state. It is commonly stated that approximately 90% of lucid dreams are DILDs and only 10% are WILDs. One problem with DILDs is it generally requires a lot of practice before you get good at inducing them. Your mind is already sleeping inside the dream and you have to learn to wake it up in order to become lucid. Another way of saying it is that you have already lost consciousness and now you must learn to get it back again. With a WILD, on the other hand, your consciousness is unbroken. There is no having to discover you're lucid. You already are right from the beginning. It takes the hit and miss out of lucid dreaming altogether. The problem is that when you lay down your mind tends to fall to sleep just as fast as your body does and it can take years of meditation and practice to become skilled at the art of keeping your mind awake and alert while you transition into sleep. It is an amazing truth that supplements that boost ACh levels can greatly assist you in this transition! This makes possible a reversal in lucid dream statistics in that when using supplements, approximately 90% of lucid dreams can be WILDs. Even if you don't attempt WILDs, the higher ACh levels increase self-awareness making it easier to recognize dream signs thereby having more DILDs.

Acetylcholine and supplements: Due to its strong role in retaining memory and keeping a nimble mind, supplements that boost ACh levels in the brain are often referred to as brain food. There are three common types of supplements available: those that form acetylcholine in the brain (ACh precursors), those that mimic the actions of acetylcholine in the brain (ACh agonist), and those that prevent the breakdown of acetylcholine in the brain (AChE inhibitors). All three can be used as a lucid dream trigger although the ACh precursors seem to be somewhat less effective than either the ACh agonist or the AChE inhibitors. All three types will be discussed in a later section.

Norepinephrine (NE): Norepinephrine (also called noradrenalin) has come to be recognized as playing a significant role in attention, focus, and memory. Specifically norepinephrine is associated with the ability to not get distracted from what you're doing and to also have a strong working memory. For people who suffer from ADD/ADHD, medications such as Ritalin are prescribed to help increase levels of norepinephrine within the brain.

With norepinephrine, more so than with the other neurotransmitters, it is especially important to distinguish between the norepinephrine that is in the brain and the norepinephrine that is in the blood. In general, norepinephrine is a brain chemical in that, the brain is where it is stored and released. However if the levels in the brain exceed a certain threshold, the norepinephrine begins to excrete from the brain and into the bloodstream where it is then carried throughout the body. This process is known as "overflow". When norepinephrine gets into the bloodstream it acts as a "flight or fight" substance. It increases our heart beat and respiratory rate, and can fill us with nervous tension.

<u>Norepinephrine and sleep:</u> Norepinephrine is normally associated with wakefulness rather than sleep. Amphetamines usually release significant amounts of norepinephrine and too much will make it very difficult to fall to sleep. This being said, one would expect that norepinephrine levels would decrease during deep sleep and increase as one moves toward wakefulness and REM. This is not quite true because the norepinephrine system essentially shuts off during typical REM sleep.

<u>Norepinephrine and dreams:</u> In general, norepinephrine is considered to be less related to dreaming than the other three types of neurotransmitters (serotonin, dopamine, and acetylcholine). Through personal experience I have found the profound effects norepinephrine can have on dreaming. Supplements that boost norepinephrine levels (in the brain) can produce similar results as acetylcholine boosting supplements. The dream experiences tend to be long and extremely vivid. Unlike acetylcholine however, norepinephrine does not seem to initiate REM sleep but rather supports its and prolongs it.

<u>Norepinephrine and lucid dreams:</u> Norepinephrine can have a profound effect on lucid dreaming. Taken in the right dose, it can act as a lucid dream trigger in the same way that acetylcholine can. Norepinephrine does more than just trigger lucid dreams however; it helps you stay extremely lucid for very long periods of time. In addition, it keeps you focused and alert while in the dream and greatly enhances the ability to recall details and memories from your waking life while within the dream. This allows you to maintain

constant attention on accomplishing any goals, experiments, or other assignments that you have prepared for the dream. There are several keys to using norepinephrine boosting supplements however. They must be used in very small doses and they are most effective if taken when naturally entering REM sleep. Since norepinephrine does not seem to initiate REM like ACh does, the two can be used together to produce an extremely effective lucid dream trigger.

Norepinephrine and supplements: There are very few non-prescription supplements that can increase norepinephrine levels without simultaneously affecting serotonin and dopamine levels. A class of substances known as alpha-2 adrenergic blockers is known to indirectly raise norepinephrine levels in the brain by preventing the binding of norepinephrine to the alpha-2 nerve cell receptors. Unfortunately, there are few natural supplements available without a prescription. One supplement that is available is a substance called Yohimbine which is very effective if taken in extremely small doses. Yohimbine will be discussed in a later chapter.

Summary: Each of these four neurotransmitters plays a crucial role in both the waking and sleep cycles, including dreaming and lucid dreaming. We can use each to our advantage in order to set up the best possible circumstances to obtain enhanced lucid dream experiences.

Serotonin: Plays an indirect role in lucid dreaming. Increasing serotonin will increase the time spent in non-REM sleep by actively suppressing REM sleep. Although the path is indirect, the serotonin system can still be used as a lucid dream aid by utilizing the REM rebound effect. Serotonin can also be used to increase the overall quality of sleep by allowing the dreamer to better balance the time spent in both non-REM and REM sleep stages.

Dopamine: Most likely plays a fundamental role in dreaming although dopamine by itself does not seem to act as a lucid dream trigger. However, dopamine greatly increases the control that a dreamer has within a lucid dream by substantially increasing confidence and motivation levels.

Acetylcholine: Plays a major role in increasing memory and promoting REM sleep. Acetylcholine can act as a lucid dream trigger by allowing the dreamer to move more easily from waking consciousness directly into a dream.

Norepinephrine: This neurotransmitter is generally thought to have much more to do with the waking state as opposed to the sleep state although my experiments have shown it to be a valuable tool for dream enhancement. Norepinephrine can act as lucid dream trigger if taken when naturally entering REM or can be used synergistically with ACh. Norepinephrine can greatly enhance focus and attention during a lucid dream. Norepinephrine also helps with remembering your waking life within the dream state and conversely your dream life within the waking state.

Part 2:

Individual Supplement Profiles

In the following chapters I shall discuss the specific over the counter supplements that have made the biggest impact on my lucid dream development. The goal of Part 2 is to introduce each of the individual supplements by summarizing their key characteristics, typical doses, possible side effects, and so on. I will also comment on the role each of these supplements has played in my lucid dream development.

In general, please exercise caution and common sense when it comes to taking dietary supplements of any kind. I strongly recommend you consult a doctor before taking supplements, especially if you have (or think you may have) any medical conditions, or are taking prescription drugs for health reasons.

6

Important Definitions

There are a few definitions and concepts that are helpful to understand. Keep in mind that not all supplements are created equal even if the labels say they do exactly the same thing. In order to help understand their usefulness, I list ten key characteristics used to compare supplements to each other and to my own goals of dream enhancement.

Blood Brain Barrier: Using supplements to enhance dreaming requires that they have some effect on the brain's chemistry. The body regulates which substances can pass into the brain through a system referred to as the "blood brain barrier". This barrier acts as a type of filter that only permits certain substances to pass from the blood into the brain. There are many substances, and therefore many supplements, that do not easily cross the blood brain barrier. These types of substances will be of little or no use in enhancing lucid dream development. Unfortunately, most of the neurotransmitters themselves do not cross this barrier and therefore taking oral doses of serotonin or dopamine, for example, will have no effect on the serotonin or dopamine levels in the brain. The supplements outlined in this book readily cross the blood brain barrier and act to increase neurotransmitter levels within the brain by using one of several mechanisms of action described below.

Mechanism of Action: Neurotransmitters, like ACh, do not easily pass through the blood brain barrier, so the supplements must be able to enter the brain and then work to increase the neurotransmitter levels. There are several mechanisms of action that the supplements can use to accomplish this. Understanding these mechanisms will help determine which supplements have the best potential of producing positive results, and give insights on how different supplements might work together synergistically to further enhance lucid dream development.

The four primary action mechanisms are the precursor, the agonist, the antagonist, and the re-uptake inhibitor.

Precursor: A precursor is a substance or component from which another substance is created. In other words a precursor is an ingredient necessary to form a different substance. For example, dopamine does not cross the blood brain barrier, but several of its precursors do. Once a dopamine precursor crosses the blood brain barrier it is utilized in the production of dopamine. Since the dopamine is now being produced inside the brain, the blood brain barrier no longer plays a role.

Each of the four neurotransmitters described in this book can be directly affected by using precursors. A general rule is that the closer the precursor is to the final product, the more efficiently it will work (assuming of course that it can pass through the blood brain barrier). The following summarizes the primary precursors of serotonin, acetylcholine, dopamine and norepinephrine.

1. Serotonin precursors:

Tryptophan → 5-HTP → Serotonin → N-Acetyl Serotonin →
Melatonin

Within the serotonin synthesis line all but serotonin
and n-Acetyl serotonin pass through the blood brain barrier
and are available as non-prescription supplements. Since 5-
HTP is closer in the chain to serotonin itself, it tends to be the
most efficient precursor at raising serotonin levels in the brain,
although Tryptophan would also be an option. As can be seen
from the diagram, elevated serotonin levels also lead to an
increase in Melatonin although since it easily passes through
the blood brain barrier, a Melatonin supplement is probably
more efficient.

2. Acetylcholine precursors:

Vitamin B5 → CoA → Acetyl
Choline Supplement → Phosphatidylcholine → Choline
Choline + Acetyl → Acetylcholine

Acetylcholine is formed by adding an acetyl group
onto a choline molecule. Vitamin B5 is the primary precursor
needed to form the acetyl group. Most normal diets include
sufficient amounts of vitamin B5 so you probably have plenty
of acetyl groups in your brain at any given time that can be

used to help form acetylcholine. This is not the case for Choline however.

Only two types of choline supplements efficiently cross the through the blood brain barrier: GPC & CDP choline. Of these two GPC is definitely the best one for lucid dream enhancement for reasons highlighted in chapter 8. Both these supplements increase levels of Phosphatidylcholine within the brain which then reverts back to choline in order to form acetylcholine.

3. Dopamine and Norepinephrine precursors

Phenylalanine → Tyrosine → L-Dopa → Dopamine →
Norepinephrine → Epinephrine

Dopamine does not pass through the blood brain barrier but all three of its precursors do. Of the three, L-dopa is by far the most efficient at increasing dopamine levels within the brain, although Phenylalanine and Tyrosine are possible alternatives. Pure L-dopa is only available by prescription but there are several species of beans that naturally contain L-dopa. The type that contains by far the highest L-dopa content is called Mucuna Pruriens. Mucuna Pruriens is available as a non-prescription supplement.

As you can see from the above diagram, dopamine is the immediate precursor to norepinephrine and therefore any precursor to dopamine is also a precursor to norepinephrine. Unlike dopamine however, norepinephrine can pass through blood brain barrier although it is available only by prescription. You wouldn't want to use it anyway because once in the blood, norepinephrine causes a host of undesirable side effects such as rapid heart beat, increased blood pressure, hypertension, and others. Norepinephrine is best kept within the brain.

Agonist: An agonist is a substance that mimics the actions of a neurotransmitter by binding to the specific receptors of the naturally occurring substance. In other words, an agonist is a totally different chemical that acts in the same way as one of the neurotransmitters. Neurotransmitters work by binding to specific types of receptors. The shape of the neurotransmitter determines whether it can fit into and bind (lock) to the receptor. You can think of a neurotransmitter as a key and a receptor as a lock. The key must have the correct shape in order to fit into and activate the lock. An agonist has essentially the same shape as the neurotransmitter and therefore can also bind to the receptor and activate it. Therefore an agonist produces the same result as the neurotransmitter itself. Unfortunately, non-prescription agonists are scarce. The only agonist I have included is Nicotine (via a patch). Nicotine is a powerful acetylcholine agonist that can produce excellent lucid dream results, but of course, has some serious drawbacks. Nicotine will be covered in detail in chapter 9.

Antagonist: An antagonist is a substance that blocks the action of another substance. In keeping with the key and lock analogy, whereas an agonist can fit into the lock and open it, an antagonist can fit into the lock but does not open it. Instead it blocks the correct key (agonist or neurotransmitter) from opening the lock. This type of action can indirectly lead to a build up of specific neurotransmitters by not letting them be utilized (used up) efficiently. Alpha-2 antagonists (sometimes called alpha-2 receptor blockers or alpha-2 adrenergic blockers) block the receptors that are normally used to control the release of norepinephrine. By blocking these receptors, the brain is tricked into thinking that there is less norepinephrine than is actually present which results in the release of additional norepinephrine within the brain. Yohimbine is an alpha-2 antagonist and will be discussed in chapter 12.

Reuptake Inhibitor: A reuptake inhibitor is a substance that prevents the breakdown of the neurotransmitter allowing it to stay in your system longer. Since the neurotransmitter is continuously being produced, a reuptake inhibitor can increase the amount of the neurotransmitter in your system by having your body create it faster than it is breaking it down. Re-uptake inhibitors are probably the doctor's favorite choice in combating a large number of mental disorders such as depression, ADD, and Alzheimer's disease. Although most re-uptake inhibitors are prescription based there are a few that are available as over the counter supplements. One of them in particular, Galantamine, is a powerful substance for lucid dream enhancement. Galantamine will be discussed in detail in chapter 7.

You should be careful with reuptake inhibitors, particularly substances called MAO inhibitors. Monoamine oxidase (MAO) is a chemical that helps break down serotonin, dopamine, and norepinephrine. Therefore a MAO inhibitor, blocks MAO from breaking down these substances leading to increases in all three neurotransmitters simultaneously (in more or less equal amounts). There are three disadvantages in using this approach for lucid dream enhancement. First, you lose direct control over how much of each individual neurotransmitter is adjusted. Secondly, you generally don't want to boost serotonin levels at the same time that you boost dopamine or norepinephrine levels. Serotonin decreases REM. Only after the serotonin wears off is it possible to experience a REM rebound effect. Thirdly, MAO inhibitors tend to cause many drug interactions which means you need to be extra careful when combining these substances with other medicines, herbs, or even some foods because it is possible to experience a potentially dangerous reaction. The reason I point this out is because MAO inhibitors are very common and are occasionally talked about by lucid dream enthusiasts. Herbs such as St. John's Wort, Passion Flower, Nutmeg, Licorice Root and many others are considered MAO inhibitors and have been sited as potential lucid dream enhancing substances. My approach is based on finding individual supplements for each of the four individual neurotransmitters and therefore I generally try to stay away from MAO inhibitors.

Summary: I have introduced four primary mechanisms of altering neurotransmitter concentrations in the brain: precursors, agonists, antagonists, and re-uptake inhibitors. We shall learn how to make use of each of these mechanisms in order to produce exceptional lucid dream experiences.

Time to peak plasma levels: After taken orally, a supplement must pass from the stomach into the blood stream. In general, the concentration of the supplement in the blood starts at zero (at the time the dose is taken), then gradually rises to some maximum concentration after a period of time, and then starts to decrease back towards zero. The time to peak plasma level is the time it takes, starting at the time you swallow the pill, for the blood concentrations to reach the maximum state. This concept is extremely important when deciding the best time to take the supplements. In general, you want the maximum concentration to be reached at the time of lucid dream induction. Some substances reach peak plasma levels in a short amount of time (i.e. less than 1 hour) while others may take much longer.

Elimination half-life: This is the amount of time it takes the plasma concentration of a supplement to be cut in half. For example, L-dopa (a precursor to dopamine) reaches its peak plasma level in 1 to 1.5 hours after ingestion. Similarly, the plasma concentration is cut in half about every ninety minutes thereafter. One hour after ingestion the peak concentration is reached; ninety minutes later the concentration is one half; another ninety minutes and the peak concentration is one quarter of its maximum level; ninety minutes later to one eighth and so on. The elimination half-life is essentially a measure of how long a substance remains in your system. As I will point out in chapter 18, in order to minimize desensitization and tolerance issues it is best to adopt of philosophy of letting the various supplements totally clear out of your system after each lucid dream attempt. By "totally clear out" I am implying that the level of each supplement has dropped to 3% or less of its maximum value.

Because of this fact, whenever possible I recommend finding supplements with short elimination half-lives.

Concentration Curve: Plotting the time to peak plasma level and elimination half life information on a curve gives a good visual representation of the relationship between time and plasma concentration for a particular supplement. These curves provide a wealth of information as we will see in the upcoming chapters. The following concentration curve is an example for Galantamine (an AChE inhibitor that boosts acetylcholine levels in the brain).

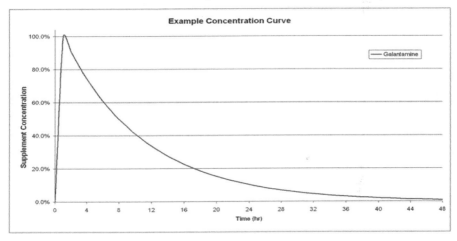

Concentration curve for Galantamine with Peak Plasma time = 1 hr and elimination half-life = 7 hr

This concentration curve visually shows how Galantamine is quickly absorbed into the blood stream and that ~48 hours are required before it is essentially cleared from the body.

Therapeutic dose The therapeutic dose is defined as the dose of a drug that is required to achieve a desired result. The therapeutic dose required for lucid dream development is generally less than the therapeutic dose associated with the more commonly cited reasons the supplements are used. This is good because side effects and drug interactions are almost always diminished at smaller doses.

Toxicity, Side Effects and the Therapeutic Index: Practically every substance known to man is toxic in large enough doses. The same is true of side effects. The important point is to understand the severity and frequency of the side effects at the therapeutic dose. The therapeutic index is one tool used to try to understand the relationship between the dose and the side effects. The therapeutic index is defined as the ratio between the minimum effective dose and maximum tolerated dose of a drug. If the therapeutic index is greater than one then few side effects occur. If the ratio is equal to or less than one then side effects will almost definitely occur. Of course another important measure is the severity of the side effects which can range from barely noticeable to life threatening.

Drug interactions: A drug interaction is defined as the action of one drug on the metabolism, effect, or toxicity of another drug. Sometimes drugs taken individually are very well tolerated but when taken together produce unwanted effects. Of course, sometimes two drugs can act harmoniously with each other and provide a greater benefit than when taken individually. Since I commonly combine supplements it is very important to be aware of any drug interactions that could occur (both good and bad). This is one reason I have tried to find supplements that more or less function on only one of the four neurotransmitters. This approach allows for better overall control and fewer interactions. As stated before, some interactions are beneficial and desired. For example the synergy that is created by combining an ACh precursor with an AChE inhibitor produces extremely good odds of triggering a lucid dream. The most important point to remember is to stay informed. Manufactures, by law, must disclose all known drug interactions. Particularly when striving for a synergistic combination, always start at low doses in order to see just how synergistic it is.

Tolerance and Desensitization: Tolerance and desensitization are related but are not synonymous with each other. Where desensitization is a physiological phenomenon, tolerance can be more of a learned phenomena. Some supplements can lead to a desensitization of the various neurotransmitter receptor sites. Should this occur, it would be necessary to take a larger dose in order to get the same effect. A larger dose leads to further desensitization which in turn requires another increase in dose. If this cycle is allowed to continue one would eventually reach the dose at which negative side effects start to occur. At this point the supplement is no longer effective.

Tolerance is a little different. For example, if someone drinks a cup of coffee before bedtime, they will most likely lie awake for several hours until the effects of the caffeine wear off. Caffeine works by blocking the action of a chemical called adenosine. Adenosine is a different type of neurotransmitter than the ones discussed in this book but it is believed to be the main sleep neurotransmitter. It has been demonstrated that caffeine, unless taken in very large doses over long periods of time, does not lead to the desensitization of adenosine receptors. Yet, if one continues to drink a cup of coffee, night after night before bedtime, eventually one starts to fall to sleep without much difficulty. This learned behavior is part of our natural adaptation process. There are also even less tangible types of tolerance. For example, the first time you take a supplement that you believe will cause lucidity, it very likely will. This is based on a strong expectation of success along with a strong emotional component. As you repeat the experiment night after night, eventually your expectations and emotions start to normalize and the supplement loses its effectiveness (even though physiologically it is still working).

Fortunately there are a few simple guidelines you can follow to avoid desensitization and tolerance. I have been very successful in not building up a tolerance or allowing desensitization to take place. This is an extremely important topic for the lucid dreamer and an entire chapter is dedicated to the methods that work best.

<u>Dream enhancement threshold and the lucidity trigger</u> : The Dream enhancement threshold (DET) is a term used to represent the effectiveness of different dosages of a particular supplement at enhancing dreams. It is a subjective measure meant to document the minimum dosage of a supplement that has an undeniable effect on dream vividness and recall. The approach is to experiment with varying dosages of a particular substance and record how the levels impact dream vividness and recall (as well as many other factors). When I reach a dose that has a positive effect on my dreaming, I flag it as having passed the DET. This information is useful in comparing the overall effectiveness of different supplements and as well as optimizing a final supplement schedule.

A lucidity trigger is another term I defined to represent the effectiveness of a particular supplement in triggering a lucid dream. Not all of the substances included in this book are lucidity triggers, nor should they be. There is more to advanced lucid dreaming than just having a lucid dream. Triggers are, of course, extremely important but so is dream control and having the ability to reason within the dream.

7

Galantamine

<u>General Description:</u> Galantamine is classified as an AChE inhibitor. Acetylcholinesterase (AChE) is the substance that breaks down acetylcholine within the brain. By inhibiting this breakdown, acetylcholine can build to increased levels. Galantamine (as well as other AChE inhibitors) is the subject of intense research because of its apparent ability to increase memory and actually improve Alzheimer's disease symptoms. Not only does Galantamine inhibit the breakdown of acetylcholine, there is also evidence that it acts as an acetylcholine agonist as well. This means that Galantamine gives a double boost to the apparent levels of ACh within the brain. Remember that acetylcholine is at its highest levels during wakefulness and REM sleep. By increasing ACh levels you will tend to go directly into REM when you fall to sleep provided that you don't put your body in conflict. The normal sleep cycle begins by moving quickly into the deeper (non-REM) stages of sleep. Taking Galantamine is not nearly as effective if taken before bedtime as opposed to after 4 or 5 hours of sleep. By taking it before bedtime you are trying to force your body into REM when it wants to enter deep sleep. Your odds of becoming lucid are greatly reduced and you are essentially depriving yourself of quality sleep.

When taken after 4 or 5 hours of sleep Galantamine can act as lucidity trigger in that it allows you to move directly from wakefulness into a dream state with an unbroken consciousness. This makes Galantamine highly effective at producing WILDs. One of the characteristics that makes Galantamine so effective is that it is rapidly absorbed by the body.

Mechanism of Action: Galantamine is an AChE (acetylcholinesterase) inhibitor. Acetylcholinesterase is the chemical that breaks down acetylcholine in the brain. Therefore Galantamine causes the acetylcholine within the brain to increase, by causing the brain to manufacture ACh faster than it is being broken down. There is some evidence suggesting that galantamine also acts as an acetylcholine agonist.

Concentration Curve: Galantamine is characterized by quick absorption and a relatively long elimination half-life. It reaches its peak plasma level just 60 minutes after ingested but takes about 48 hours to be completely flushed from you system.

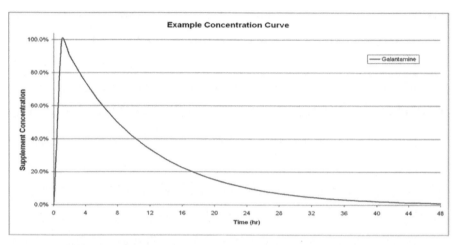

Concentration curve for Galantamine with Peak Plasma time=1hr and elimination half-life =7hr

Effect on Dreams: Galantamine has a profound impact on dreaming. Galantamine will cause extremely vivid and long dreams. If the Galantamine is allowed to fully clear from your system (i.e. only take it every other night or less) dreams seem to be normal and pleasant (especially if using Piracetam to counter desensitization – see chapter 10). If Galantamine is not allowed to completely clear out of the body and/or if tolerance/desensitization starts to occur, dreams can become more movie like, bazaar, and perhaps nightmarish (kind of like morbid Picasso images). This is an excellent marker that you need to take some time off from using the substance and from stimulating the cholinergic system in general. This can be totally avoided if lucid dream attempts are kept to an every other day basis or less and if Piracetam is used to counter the effects of Galantamine directly following a lucid dream attempt (see chapters 10 & 18).

Effect on Lucid Dreams: As I have mentioned, Galantamine can be used as a lucid dream trigger. There are several other substances that can also trigger lucidity (Nicotine, GPC, and small doses of Yohimbine) but I tend to favor Galantamine for a number of reasons.

<u>Side Effects:</u> There are numerous side effects listed for Galantamine: Nausea, vomiting, diarrhea, dizziness, decreased appetite and weight loss. These are all dose related however. Due to its positive impact on memory, Galantamine is commonly taken to reduce the effects of Alzheimer's disease at doses up to 24 mg per day. Lucid dream enthusiast will find that no more than 8 mg are necessary to trigger a lucid dream. At the 8 mg dose level that I use I have noticed three main side effects:

1. I get some strange noises coming from my stomach. This is more interesting than annoying.
2. It is possible to get muscle cramps and/or spasms. There have been several occasions where I wake up after a lucid dream and when I stand up I get an immediate charley horse in one or both of my calves. This has happened maybe 2 or 3 percent of the time. The cramps go away quickly but the muscle can feel tense for more than a day following a cramp.
3. Energy drained on the following day. Galantamine will give a considerable boost to your cholinergic system and can in turn deprive you of the deep rejuvenating sleep stages. It is much better to take Galantamine after about 4 or 5 hours of sleep. This will greatly improve your odds of becoming lucid and also allow your body to get the deep sleep it needs in the first part of the night. This can be further enhanced by taking 5-HTP prior to going to sleep. The 5-HTP suppresses REM in the first half of the night and is just about worn off when

Galantamine is taken. Galantamine suppresses deep sleep in the second half of the night. The result is a more or less balanced night's sleep. This approach has made a huge difference in how I feel following a night using Galantamine.

Dosage: I have almost exclusively used 8 mg capsules. More than that is not necessary and should be avoided in order to minimize tolerance/desensitization and avoid any negative side effects. I have also experimented with 4 mg and still experienced extremely vivid dreams although I currently use 8 mg regularly.

Special Notes: Notice that Galantamine remains in your system for about 48 hours. This means that your acetylcholine levels are boosted well beyond the time you set aside for lucid dreaming. This can lead to tolerance and desensitization issues. One can avoid this if they follow the detailed schedule laid out in chapters 17, 18, & 19.

There are several forms of Galantamine available: pure Galantamine, Galantamine combined with a form Choline; and Galantamine combined with other supplements. For reasons that will become clear in the next chapter, I recommend combining Galantamine with Choline either as a pre-formulated mixture or taken individually. Try to avoid purchasing Galantamine that is pre-mixed with supplements other than Choline.

Also be aware that there is another AChE inhibitor that is available without a prescription. This substance is Huperzine A and has been used in Chinese medicine for a very long time. At the present time I have not done any experiments with this substance but it may be an alternative to galantamine.

Summary: I use Galantamine as a lucid dream trigger. For this to work Galantamine should be taken after 4 or 5 hours of quality deep sleep. Since Galantamine takes a full 48 hours to completely clear out of your system, it should not be taken on two consecutive nights. If dreams become movie like and/or bazaar consider taking a few days off. Piracetam can be used directly following a lucid dream attempt to counteract the effects of Galantamine and reduce sensitivity to tolerance and/or desensitization.

Galantamine Summary Table	
Mechanism of action	AChE inhibitor (prevents breakdown of acetylcholine. Also may act as an ACh agonist
Able to cross the blood brain barrier	Yes
Time to peak plasma levels	1 hour
Elimination half-life	7 hours
Maximum daily dose	24 mg (for treatment of Alzheimer's disease)
Lucid dream dose	8 mg or less
Effect on dreams	Extremely vivid and long
Effect on Lucid dreams	Can be used as a lucid dream trigger

8

Choline Supplements

<u>General Description:</u> Choline is very closely related to the vitamin B family and is considered an essential nutrient by the US Food and Drug Administration (FDA). There are many kinds of Choline supplements available: Choline Salts (Choline Citrate & Choline Bitartrate), Lecithin (phosphatidylcholine), CDP-Choline, GPC (Glycerophosphocholine), and others. Of the available forms, the Choline salts and GPC have proven to be especially useful for lucid dream enhancement.

Choline Salts:

Both Choline Bitartrate and Choline Citrate are part of group of substances referred to as Choline salts. When you see a supplement that is simply called Choline, most likely it is either the bitartrate or citrate variety. These two types are the most common and most in-expensive forms of Choline supplement available. Although the salts pass through the blood brain barrier, it is often said that they do so inefficiently. Their transport is controlled by the concentration gradient between the blood and the brain and normally the brain has high enough concentrations of Choline to allow only a small fraction of the supplements to enter. However if brain concentrations are lower, Choline is transported more efficiently.

Once in the brain, free Choline is quickly converted into acetylcholine and therefore low levels of Choline translate into low levels of ACh and visa versa.   Since during the non-REM stages of sleep, acetylcholine levels are lower than normal, transport of free Choline is improved if available.

The advantage that the Choline salts have is that they are more quickly absorbed by the body. This allows them to be used synergistically with Galantamine. In addition to the overall level of ACh in the brain, an important factor in initiating a WILD is the rate of increase of acetylcholine. Galantamine inhibits the breakdown of ACh but does not increase the production of it. Adding one of the salts can jump start the accumulation process by producing ACh at a faster rate. This noticeably increases the odds of becoming lucid and can intensify the transitioning process (see chapter 22) from what is normally experienced with Galantamine alone.

GPC:

Although the Choline salts can jump start the accumulation process, they quickly lose there efficiency as the concentration of ACh increases. To keep the accumulation process going, a different type of supplement is required; one that does not depend on low levels of ACh. Only two types of Choline supplements are known to cross the blood brain barrier efficiently under normal conditions: CDP-choline and GPC. Both supplements act as a precursor to acetylcholine, but of the two, GPC is superior when it comes to lucid dream enhancement. There are three reasons GPC is preferred:

1. The time to peak plasma levels for GPC is 3 hours. Whereas the time to peak plasma levels of CDP-choline is 6 hours.

2. The elimination half life of GPC is ~ 1.5 hours. The elimination half life of CDP choline is ~4.5 hours.

3. I have successfully used GPC as a lucid dream trigger but CDP-choline has never triggered a lucid dream for me or even had much of an impact on dreaming at all. Also GPC works synergistically with Galantamine to give excellent odds of becoming lucid whereas CDP-choline didn't have any noticeable impact.

If you are trying to increase your memory, both supplements may work the same. However, if you are trying to develop high quality lucid dreams, GPC has clear advantages. The fact that CDP-choline has such a long time until the peak plasma levels are reached makes it far from ideal for the lucid dreamer. To use CDP-choline, one would most likely need to take it before bedtime so the peak plasma levels would arrive at the time of the lucid dream attempt. Although this may seem like a viable approach, consider what is happening to the quality of deep sleep in the hours before the attempt. Acetylcholine levels would be slowly and steadily rising while the body is trying to maintain the low levels needed for the deep rejuvenating sleep stages. The result is a decrease in sleep quality.

GPC stands for Glycerophosphocholine but it has also been called Choline Alfoscerate, Alphoscerate, L-alpha-Glycerylphosphorylcholine, and alpha-GPC. GPC has been used extensively in Italy and other parts of Europe but has only recently become available in the United States. Due to this fact, most of the research has come out of Europe. The European research is very impressive and GPC has been shown to improve cognitive function for both young and old in several studies. Some studies have shown GPC to be just as effective as Donezepil and superior to Rivastigmine (both are prescription AChE inhibitors) in relieving the symptoms of Alzheimer's disease. Furthermore GPC is extremely well tolerated and has no serious side effects at the therapeutic dosages.

Mechanism of Action: Choline supplements are precursors to acetylcholine and cause acetylcholine levels to rise by allowing the brain to produce more.

Concentration Curve: Because Choline is found naturally in many food sources, it has been difficult to find peak plasma time studies for the standard forms (i.e. the Choline salts). Several studies suggest that the Choline salts are metabolized faster than the other forms (GPC and CDP). One study mentions that Choline Bitartrate is absorbed more than twice as fast as fast as GPC and has the same elimination half life. GPC has an elimination half life of 90 minutes and takes about 3 hours to reach its peak plasma levels. Based on this information, I have assumed that Choline Bitartrate reaches peak plasma times in about an hour and also has a 90 minute elimination half life. Due to the similarity in structure and metabolic pathways it is probable that Choline Citrate is metabolized in the same way as Choline Bitartrate.

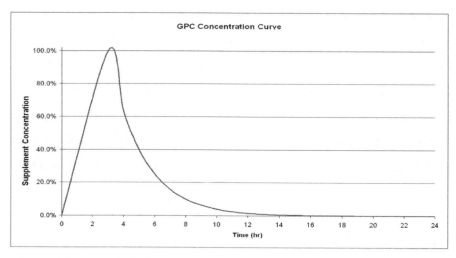

Concentration curve for GPC with Peak Plasma time = 3 hr and elimination half-life = 1.5 hr

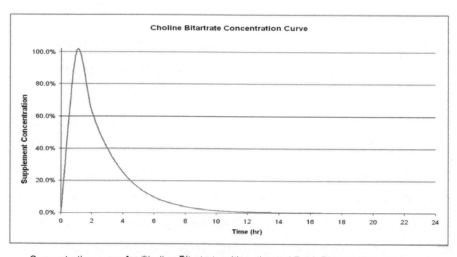

Concentration curve for Choline Bitartrate with estimated Peak Plasma time = 1 hr and elimination half-life = 1.5 hr

<u>Effect on Dreams:</u> GPC has a profound impact on dreaming and causes dreams to be exceptionally vivid and long. I have not had any bazaar or nightmarish dreams using GPC but have not tried it without following up with Piracetam to avoid desensitization issues.

Choline salts do not have much of an impact on dreaming unless they are combined with Galantamine in which case they can intensify the action of Galantamine.

Effect on Lucid Dreams: Combining a Choline salt with Galantamine increases the odds of experiencing a WILD. I consider the Galantamine/Choline combination to be the fundamental lucidity trigger from which all others are derived.

GPC has a profound effect on lucid dreaming and can be used either as a trigger or as a support for Galantamine. If it is used as a trigger, it has the advantage that it is easier to fall back to sleep than when using either Galantamine or Yohimbine. This is primarily due to the longer time it takes to reach peak plasma levels. The negative side of this is it does not lend itself as well to WILDs and all my lucid dreams using GPC by itself have been DILDs.

When using Galantamine/Choline and GPC together I have a very high success rate in becoming lucid. This combination works incredibly synergistically together. Interestingly this combination also has a tendency to give my lucid dreams a soundtrack in that I hear music playing (sometimes very loudly) during the dream. Nicotine (an ACh agonist) has a similar effect but of course also has some serious drawbacks (see chapter 9).

Side Effects: Both types of supplements are extremely well tolerated. Most GPC studies available report only mild side effects in a small percentage of the people taking the supplement. The side effects generally included nausea and insomnia. I have no noticeable side effect with doses up to 1200 mg of GPC or with up to 1000 mg of a Choline salt.

Dosage: The dosage used for most of the GPC studies was 1200 mg taken once daily. I have taken GPC by itself at doses of 900 mg and 1200 mg and have combined it with Galantamine at doses of 600 mg, 900 mg, and 1200 mg. I have had lucid dreams under all of these conditions, but the 900 mg dose had less success than the 1200 mg dose when GPC was taken alone.

Choline is considered an essential nutrient and the recommended daily allowance is 425 mg/day for women and 550 mg/day for men. The maximum safe level of Choline has been set at 3.5 grams/day. For lucid dream enhancement 400 – 800 mg should be sufficient. I typically use 500 mg of Choline Bitartrate in combination with 8 mg of Galantamine.

When adding GPC to the Galantamine/Choline mix, a 600 mg dose of GPC improves the odds of becoming lucid and noticeably increases the length of the lucid dream. At doses of 900 mg and 1200 mg I experienced intense periods of acceleration (see chapter 22) and music playing during my lucid dreams. The music seems to be louder with the 1200 mg dose.

Special Notes: In order to form acetylcholine two ingredients are needed: Choline + Acetyl. Choline supplements provide the Choline but where does your body get the Acetyl group from? The answer is from vitamin B5. Most diets include plenty of vitamin B5 but it is probably not a bad idea to supplement your diet with a good multivitamin taken in the morning (not at the time of a lucid dream attempt). I did some experiments taking vitamin B5 in the form of Panteteine (activated form of B5) at the time of the lucid dream attempt but I don't recommend it; it makes it very hard to fall to sleep and my other experiments have shown that I don't need it (although I do get B5 in my regular diet).

Vitamin B5 → CoA → Acetyl

GPC→ phosphatidylcholine → Choline

Choline + Acetyl → Acetylcholine

Summary: GPC and the Choline salts (bitartrate and citrate) are excellent supplements to support lucid dreaming. Combining a Choline salt with Galantamine increases the odds of experiencing a WILD and is the foundation of all other combinations described in this book. GPC can be used to trigger lucid dreams although I generally experience DILDs instead of WILDs when I use GPC alone. My favorite way to use GPC is in combination with Galantamine/Choline taken 4 or 5 hours after going to bed. When I use GPC this way I find 600 mg is optimum (although I occasionally use 900 mg). GPC and Galantamine/Choline give me a high success rate at becoming lucid. Note, I do not use them on consecutive nights and use Piracetam immediately following my lucid dreams (see chapter 10). Both GPC and the Choline salts are extremely well tolerated and have few noticeable side effects.

Choline Salt (Bitartrate & Citrate) Summary Table	
Mechanism of action	Precursors to Acetylcholine
Able to cross the blood brain barrier	Yes, but only efficiently when brain has low levels of ACh (as in non-REM or early REM sleep)
Time to peak plasma levels	Estimated at 1 hour
Elimination half-life	1.5 hours
Maximum daily dose	3500 mg
Lucid dream dose	400 - 800 mg in combination with Galantamine
Effect on dreams	Supports Galantamine to increase dream vividness and recall.
Effect on Lucid dreams	Used synergistically with Galantamine

GPC Summary Table	
Mechanism of action	Precursors to Acetylcholine
Able to cross the blood brain barrier	Yes
Time to peak plasma levels	3 hours
Elimination half-life	1.5 hours
Maximum daily dose	Some studies used up to 3000 mg but most studies used 1200 mg.
Lucid dream dose	600-1200 mg
Effect on dreams	Causes vivid and long dreams
Effect on Lucid dreams	Can be used as a lucid dream trigger, can be synergistically with Galantamine

9

Nicotine

General Description: Nicotine is a very controversial substance. Personally I only use Nicotine on rare occasion, but it was one of the first substances I experimented with, and because I have had some profound results, it must be included here in order to be complete. Nicotine is available via a patch or chewing gum as an over the counter aid to help quit smoking. Nicotine acts as an acetylcholine agonist which means it has essentially the same effects as acetylcholine inside the brain and it quickly and efficiently crosses the blood brain barrier. Although Nicotine does not cause cancer, it is addictive when used regularly and is toxic even in small doses. More importantly, Nicotine causes both short term and long term desensitization of the acetylcholine receptors and since these receptors are crucial for lucid dreaming it is wise not to take this fact lightly. Warnings aside, Nicotine can have a profound effect on lucid dreaming when used (1) on rare occasions (2) in small doses and (3) when a proactive method is utilized to counteract desensitization. Nicotine produces effects similar to GPC in that it can be used to trigger lucid dreams and it also works synergistically with Galantamine. Although my experience has shown that Nicotine is significantly more effective than GPC, Nicotine can have far greater side effects so greater care must be taken in controlling the dose.

<u>Mechanism of Action:</u> Nicotine is an agonist for acetylcholine which means that it enters the brain and acts in the same manner as acetylcholine.

<u>Concentration Curve:</u> If Nicotine is administered via a patch, the concentration curve looks somewhat different than those of orally administered supplements. When a patch is applied, plasma levels of Nicotine rises fairly linearly until the peak plasma levels are reached and then slowly drops over the remainder of the day (while the patch is effective), and then drops much more quickly after the patch is removed.

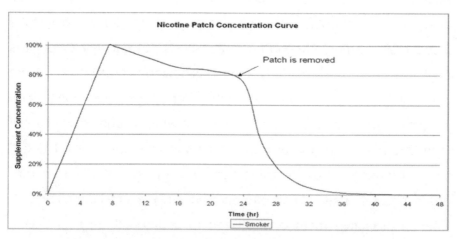

Concentration curve for a Nicotine Patch when used for an anti-smoking aid.

Although this is a typical curve for a user who is trying to quit smoking it is not a typical curve for someone who only uses a Nicotine patch to promote lucid dreaming. Because of the rapid desensitization that can occur when using Nicotine it is wise to only wear the patch during the lucid dream attempt and then remove it immediately. For example, the patch can be applied at 4 AM just prior to having an LD and then removed at 7 AM just after waking up from the lucid dream. This approach is a must if you want to be able to consistently achieve remarkable results. The following concentration curve compares the typical user to the lucid dream enthusiast.

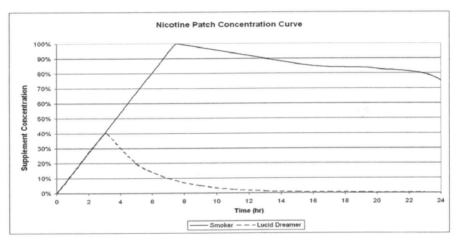

Concentration curve for Nicotine Patch for use as a lucid dream supplement

Nicotine (via the patch) is characterized by relatively slow absorption (~7.5 hours to reach peak plasma levels) countered with a short elimination half-life (~2 hours).

Effect on Dreams: Nicotine has a profound impact on dreaming. Non-lucid Nicotine dreams seem a bit more disturbing than those produced by either GPC or Galantamine and the visual vividness is sometimes lacking.

<u>Effect on Lucid Dreams:</u> Although Nicotine can trigger lucid dreams by itself it is incredibly effective when combined with Galantamine. If I had one word to describe the influence of Nicotine on my lucid dreams it would be "music". Especially when Nicotine is combined with Galantamine, my lucid dreams seem to have a soundtrack full of wonderful and totally original music.

<u>Side Effects:</u> Of all the supplements I have tried, Nicotine has the worst side effects. These can be managed however, if the patch is low dose and only worn during the lucid dream attempt. In general, too much Nicotine makes you feel ill. The side effects generally listed are: dizziness, nausea, sore throat, dry or watering mouth, watering eyes, headache, constipation, and skin irritation (where patch is worn). When I first started using Nicotine as a lucid dream aid I would put the patch on prior to going to bed. After a full eight hours of wearing the patch I would feel and look sick. My complexion was literally green. This went away however when I started putting the patch on at around 4 AM and then removing it at about three hours later. Not only did the side effects go away but I had better results and better quality of sleep.

<u>Dosage:</u> Nicotine patches typically come in three strengths: 7 mg, 14mg, and 21 mg. I have tried the 14 mg and 7 mg variety. They both work well but the 7 mg results in far fewer side effects. The dose generally represents the average total dose released over a 24 hour period (or 16 hour period depending on the brand).

Special Notes: A possible alternative to Nicotine patches is Nicotine gum. The gum gives a larger dose in a shorter period of time but wears off faster. I have not done any experimentation with Nicotine gum.

Summary: Nicotine does not cause cancer (the tar in cigarettes is the culprit there) however it is addictive and extremely toxic for small children and pets. Practically speaking, if you were to use a Nicotine patch solely as an aid for lucid dreaming, you would most likely never become addicted and if you take proper care in keeping the patches away from children you will not need to worry about accidentally poisoning anybody. If you use the lowest dose patch (7 mg) and keep it on for only a few hours you most likely will not notice any serious side effects. There is an important reason not to use Nicotine very often however, and that is because is causes rapid desensitization of your nicotinic receptors (one type of acetylcholine receptor): definitely not for everyday (or even once a week usage). Personally, I rarely use Nicotine these days because of this fact and because GPC produces similar results. I will admit that Nicotine can have a profound effect on the ability to have lucid dreams. If you are going to consider using Nicotine I strongly recommend that you follow up by using the nootropic Piracetam (see the next chapter) in order to help counteract desensitization.

Nicotine Summary Table	
Mechanism of action	Acetylcholine Agonist
Able to cross the blood brain barrier	Yes
Time to peak plasma levels	7.5 hours if wearing a patch
Elimination half-life	2 hours (after patch is removed)
Maximum daily dose	21 mg is max strength available but may lead to significant side effects
Lucid dream dose	7 mg patch applied after 4-5 hours of sleep
Effect on dreams	Vivid, long, and frequently disturbing
Effect on Lucid dreams	Can be used as a lucid dream trigger, can be synergistically with Galantamine

10

Piracetam

General Description: Piracetam is a very important substance the lucid dreamer has at their disposal, but not for the reasons you might think. Piracetam does not enhance dreaming (or lucid dreaming) at all; in fact it has proven to significantly suppress dreaming. If you would like to prove this to yourself take a healthy dose of Piracetam along with Galantamine (which has a profound effect on dreaming) and see if you can even remember having any dreams. Piracetam however, reduces desensitization of the acetylcholine receptors and for this reason it allows for more frequent lucid dream attempts when used correctly.

Piracetam is in a class of drugs called Nootropics. Nootropics are typically defined as "smart" drugs because they are believed to have a positive impact on your brain as well as on your ability to think and remember. They are also defined as having an extremely low toxicity which means that they are safe to take even in large doses. Not all Nootropics are created equal however and Piracetam is the only one that I have found in which there is an abundant amount research on how it affects the cholinergic system (acetylcholine). Piracetam is thought to cause acetylcholine to be used up more efficiently and may even increase acetylcholine receptor density.

Furthermore Piracetam has been shown to counteract the desensitization of the nicotinic receptors when carbachol is used (a powerful ACh agonist that quickly desensitizes ACh receptors). This makes Piracetam an extremely powerful tool for two reasons:

1. Both Galantamine and GPC boost acetylcholine levels and stay in your system well beyond the time it takes to attempt a lucid dream. It is best to counteract this effect as soon as the lucid dream attempt has ended. Piracetam allows you to do this. (See chapter 18 for details).
2. Nicotine is known to cause both short term and long term desensitization of the nicotinic receptors. Piracetam has been shown to counteract this desensitization.

Another advantage to using Piracetam is that while it is protecting your acetylcholine receptors so you can keep having high level dreams, there is evidence that it makes you smarter while doing so. Piracetam has been widely used and studied in Europe and Asia; however the US has done fairly little research. The FDA has not approved Piracetam but that doesn't mean it is illegal to buy in the US. It is perfectly legal to purchase up to a three month supply of Piracetam for your own use and there are several US companies that currently stock it. I have included several articles in the reference section you should read to learn about all of the benefits of Piracetam.

Keep in mind one extremely important point. It is best to not have any Piracetam in your system at the time of lucid dream attempt. This will be explained in detail in Part 3 of this book.

<u>Concentration Curve:</u> Piracetam is characterized by quick absorption and a relatively long elimination half-life. Piracetam is more or less completely out of your system after about 30 hours. This information is important to understand because Piracetam should not be in your system at the time of a lucid dream attempt.

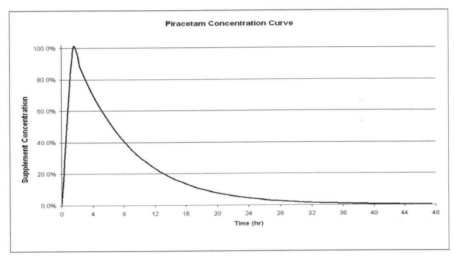

Concentration curve for Piracetam with Peak Plasma time=1.5hr and elimination half-life=5hr

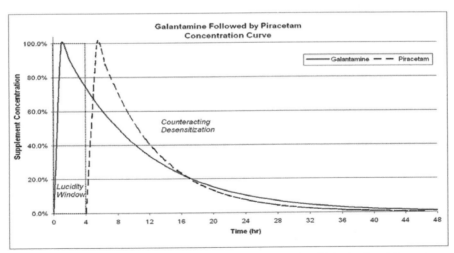

Concentration curve for Piracetam & Galantamine overlapping (Galantamine at time = 0, followed by single dose of Piracetam at time = 4 hrs)

Effect on Dreams: Inhibits dreaming and remembering dreams. Piracetam is not used to enhance dreaming but rather to counteract desensitization and tolerance caused by the other acetylcholine boosting supplements.

Effect on Lucid Dreams: Piracetam has a negative impact on lucid dreaming if it is in your system at the time of the attempt. It is the only substance that I know of that has been clinically proven to counteract desensitization. When used correctly it can increase the frequency at which you can attempt a lucid dream using the Galantamine, GPC, and/or Nicotine.

Side Effects: Piracetam, as with most nootropics, is known as having an almost total lack of toxicity. This means it causes no significant side effects even at extremely high doses. If a large dose is taken however (more than 3000 mg in a day), it is recommended to ramp down the dosage rather than to abruptly stop taking it. Piracetam increases blood flow to your brain and if you take a large single dose you may experience a headache when it wears off due to the re-constricting of the blood vessels. This can be totally avoided if the dose is spread out and ramped down instead of taking a single large dose. See chapter 18 for more details about how to take Piracetam.

Dosage: Most references call out a daily dose of 2400 - 4800 mg per day as a maximum recommended dose. The maximum dose does not correspond to the dose at which negative side effects occur but rather to the maximum dose that seems to benefit the user. There have been several studies that show that taking more than 4800mg of Piracetam produces less positive effects on memory. Furthermore the optimum dose may be age related. One study showed that the optimum dose for younger people was 2400 mg/day and was 4800 mg/day for older people. Human studies have been done with daily doses up to 20 grams per day and animal studies have been with huge dose/weight ratios. I typically take 2400 mg in a single dose immediately following a lucid dream attempt. This allows me to successfully counteract tolerance and desensitization and does not lead to a headache.

Special Notes: The FDA has not approved the use of Piracetam as a means of combating mental illnesses. This does not mean US doctors dispute the effects Piracetam has on the cholinergic system. These studies are well documented. The FDA also does not claim that Piracetam has any negative side effects. The lack of approval corresponds with the belief that there is not enough evidence to show that Piracetam works as a viable means of combating certain mental illnesses. As lucid dreamers, our primary goal is to guard against desensitization and tolerance; any mental enhancements are a fringe benefit. The fact that the FDA has not approved Piracetam may be a blessing in disguise because if the FDA were to approve Piracetam it would most likely be available by prescription only. Also Piracetam is part of a family of substances called racetams. All of the racetams work in similar way and therefore other family members, such as Aniracetam and Oxiracetam, may also guard against desensitization and tolerance effects. Of the three however, I have found more clinical research pertaining to Piracetam regarding its positive effects on cholinergic system.

Summary: Piracetam plays an important yet indirect role in lucid dream development. It is used to counteract the desensitization that may occur when using other cholinergic supplements such as Galantamine, GPC, and Nicotine. It is important not have Piracetam in your system at the time of a lucid dream attempt. It is also important to ramp down the dosage to avoid experiencing a headache if large daily doses are taken. The details of how to properly use Piracetam are covered in chapter 18.

Piracetam Summary Table	
Mechanism of action	Enhances ACh synthesis
Able to cross the blood brain barrier	Yes
Time to peak plasma levels	1.5 hours
Elimination half-life	5 hours
Maximum daily dose	Doses up to 20 grams have been used with no side effects (ramp down necessary to avoid headache)
Lucid dream dose	2400-4800 mg/day **following** lucid dream attempt (see chapter 18)
Effect on dreams	Suppresses dreams
Effect on Lucid dreams	Used to counteract desensitization which allows for more frequent lucid dream attempts

11

Mucuna Pruriens

General Description: Mucuna Pruriens is a bean producing plant that has been used in Ayurveda (Indian medicine) for over 4500 years. This is one of the few known plants that naturally contains a chemical called L-dopa. Although dopamine does not cross the blood brain barrier, L-dopa does and it is the immediate precursor to dopamine. This fact makes Mucuna Pruriens highly effective at increasing dopamine levels within the brain. There are many of reasons to supplement your diet with a little L-dopa even if you aren't interested in lucid dreaming. Dopamine is vitally important in sustaining your motor skills and as we age our dopamine levels drop significantly. Parkinson disease is an extreme case of this in which movement is severely restricted due to the loss of proper dopamine functionality. The first line of defense in Parkinson disease is L-dopa. Supplementing your diet with L-dopa containing substances can help keep you active and feeling young. In addition, dopamine makes you feel good and plays a major role in developing confidence and motivation. So even if lucid dreams aren't your goal, L-dopa containing supplements can probably do you some good. Of course when it comes to dreaming, dopamine plays a major role in that it is believed the dopamine network must be engaged for dreaming to occur in the first place.

When it comes to lucid dreaming L-dopa (via Mucuna Pruriens) boosts your ability to control the dream like no other substance I've encountered.

Mucuna Pruriens offers another benefit over the synthetic L-dopa that is commonly prescribed in the US. Synthetic L-dopa must be taken with a different chemical called Carbidopa. Carbidopa is required to keep the L-dopa from being synthesized into dopamine before it crosses the blood barrier. Since dopamine can not cross this barrier, if the L-dopa is converted to dopamine too early it does not make it into the brain and therefore does you no good. Furthermore, the negative side effects of L-dopa are typically due to the dopamine that is created in the gut rather than in the brain. Mucuna Pruriens does not require Carbidopa for reasons that are not fully understood, but there are numerous studies showing that Mucuna Pruriens is as effective as the synthetic L-dopa / Carbidopa pair. This allows for lower doses of L-dopa resulting in a lower chance of negative side effects.

Mechanism of Action: Mucuna Pruriens naturally contains the chemical L-dopa. L-dopa is the immediate precursor to dopamine. Increasing the amount of L-dopa in the brain leads to an increase in the production of dopamine.

Concentration Curve: Mucuna Pruriens is characterized by quick absorption and a short elimination half-life. It reaches its peak plasma levels just 90 minutes after you take it and is practically out of your system after 12 hours.

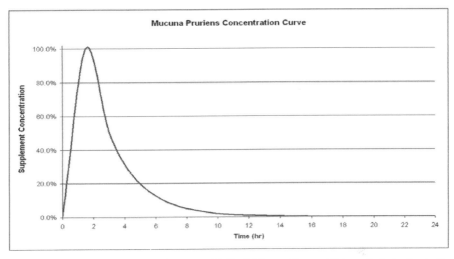

Concentration curve for Mucuna Pruriens with Peak Plasma time = 1.5 hr and elimination half-life = 1.5 hr

Effect on Dreams: L-dopa in known to cause vivid dreams and so does Mucuna Pruriens. In general however, the dose needs to be in the therapeutic range for treating Parkinson's disease before a major impact on dreaming is observed. My own experiments have shown that around 400 mg of L-dopa (via Mucuna Pruriens) are needed to stimulate a dopamine dream. Dopamine dreams are fascinating and are my personal favorite type of non-lucid dream. They are always extremely action packed and fully participatory (meaning that the dreamer is fully caught up in the action rather than just observing it). There seems to a common theme to dopamine dreams: the dreamer is put in some kind of threatening situation and must overcome some type of adversary. On the outside, these dreams often sound like nightmares, but on the inside they are usually characterized by a strong feeling of confidence and a triumphant rush once the dreamer has prevailed. I find these types of dreams thoroughly enjoyable although they may not be for everybody.

Effect on Lucid Dreams: The effect of Mucuna Pruriens on lucid dreaming is indirect yet profound. Mucuna Pruriens does not act as a lucid dream trigger. Furthermore if a large dose of Mucuna is taken with Galantamine, the odds of becoming lucid seem to be somewhat reduced. There are some studies that suggest that L-dopa can actually suppress REM. However, if a small dose of Mucuna is taken with Galantamine (or one of the other triggers) or if larger doses are taken some time before the trigger, the results are almost unbelievable. The dopamine boost that is caused by Mucuna Pruriens leads to a significant increase in confidence level. This increase in confidence leads to a total lack of fear and a profound boost in the ability to control the dream.

There are no other supplements I have found that have this effect. Advanced flying is possible, moving through walls or other objects seems incredibly natural, and changing your dreamscape is made much easier.

Side Effects: Mucuna Pruriens is new to the West but has been used for centuries in other parts of the world. High doses of Mucuna Pruriens can cause over stimulation, increased body temperature, insomnia, and nausea. There are some studies that suggest it may lead to an increased risk of birth defects so it should not be taken when pregnant.

Dosage: There is no daily suggested dose for Mucuna Pruriens although most companies list a suggested dose of 200-300 mg of L-dopa per day (the corresponding Mucuna dosage depends on the %

standardization). There is an important rule of thumb that can be used to define the maximum allowable dose. Parkinson disease patients are often on massive doses of L-dopa and it is well known that after several years of treatment they are subject to a condition referred to as dyskinesias. Dyskinesias is a condition described by sudden, involuntary, jerky movements. Most physicians now cap the maximum dose of L-dopa at no more than 600 mg/day and if possible keep the dose at 400 mg or lower over the first 3-5 years in order to reduce the risk of dyskinesias. Typically I use 80-200 mg of L-dopa (via Mucuna Pruriens) in combination with other supplements for the purpose of lucid dream enhancement.

Special Notes: Mucuna Pruriens is available in seed form or as standardized extracts. The seeds can vary substantially from seed to seed as to the concentration of L-dopa so I don't recommend using them. The standardized extracts are available in 10%, 30%, and 50% L-dopa concentrations. I strongly recommend the lower concentrations. I have tried both the 10% and 50% forms and have much better results with the 10% extract at equivalent L-dopa doses. Remember that synthetic L-dopa is prescribed with Carbidopa in order to keep the L-dopa from prematurely synthesizing into dopamine. Mucuna Pruriens has proven to be effective without the use of Carbidopa. As the concentration of L-dopa increases, the concentration of the other compounds that mimic the Carbidopa decrease and you are prone to more negative side effects and less impact on dreaming. This knowledge is from personal experience. At 500 mg of L-dopa I have experienced vivid dreams and no side effects using the 10% form, but at the same dose using the 50% form I suffered nausea and noticed no impact on dreaming.

Vitamin B6 should not be taken simultaneously with Mucuna Pruriens (or any L-dopa containing substance). Vitamin B6 is the ingredient necessary to synthesize L-dopa into dopamine. If there are large amounts of B6 present in your digestive track when you take Mucuna, the L-dopa may be converted too early and hence not be able to cross the blood brain barrier.

<u>Summary:</u> Mucuna Pruriens does not act as a lucid dream trigger but can greatly increase control when combined with Galantamine or other lucid dream triggers. Superman style flying, moving through objects, and changing the dreamscape all become much more natural, straight forward and easy when 80-200 mg of L-dopa (via Mucuna Pruriens) is taken with Galantamine (or 1 hour prior – see chapter 19 for details). No other supplement that I have found has made such a large impact on dream control as Mucuna Pruriens.

Mucuna Pruriens Summary Table	
Mechanism of action	Source of L-dopa (precursor to dopamine)
Able to cross the blood brain barrier	Yes
Time to peak plasma levels	1.5 hours
Elimination half-life	1.5 hours
Maximum daily dose	Up to 400 mg of L-dopa daily is considered safe.
Lucid dream dose	80-200 mg of L-dopa combined with Galantamine (or other trigger)
Effect on dreams	Action Packed, vivid, and long
Effect on Lucid dreams	Boosts confidence resulting in enhanced dream control and reduced fear in difficult situations

12

Yohimbine

General Description: Yohimbine is probably the most controversial substance I regularly use. Yohimbine is the primary active ingredient in Yohimbe Bark which is a tree native to Africa. Although it was initially used by weightlifters to increase blood flow during a workout, it is primarily used today to combat male impotence. Although Yohimbine is classified as a mild MAO (Monoamine Oxidase) inhibitor, its main function is as an alpha-2 adrenergic antagonist. This function blocks norepinephrine from binding with alpha-2 receptors and results in an increase in norepinephrine levels in the brain. At the dose typically taken for impotence, the levels of norepinephrine build up so much in the brain that a phenomenon occurs referred to as overflow. Overflow is the process where norepinephrine flows from the brain through the blood brain barrier and into the bloodstream. It is the high levels of norepinephrine in the blood (not the brain) that can be used be to counteract impotence but also cause a host of negative side effects. Keep in mind that another name for norepinephrine is noradrenalin which is the direct precursor to adrenaline (also called epinephrine). These substances are referred to as fight or flight substances because they are responsible for that nervous tension you get right before a confrontation.

When in the blood it is common to experience sweaty palms and feet, increased heart rate and pressure, butterflies in your stomach, a slight ache in your joints, anxiousness, and so on. As lucid dream enthusiasts we neither need nor want for overflow to occur. This requires a significant reduction in dose from what is commonly used. When in the brain, norepinephrine improves mood, alertness, focus, as well as working memory and has proven to have profound effect on dreaming and lucid dreaming. I have found the ideal dose to be ~1/20 of the dose typically found in single pill. Since my lucid dreaming method consists of attempts on an every other day basis, it would take over a month before I would use up a single dose (assuming that I used Yohimbine on every attempt, which I don't). At these small doses two facts stand out: (1) I suffer no negative side effects and (2) the effect on dreaming and lucid dreaming is profound. Another misconception is that Yohimbine is a male only herb. This is not the case and studies have shown that Yohimbine has essentially the same effects on men and women with no increase in risk.

Mechanism of Action: Yohimbine is an alpha-2 adrenergic antagonist. The alpha-2 receptors are responsible for controlling the production of norepinephrine within the brain. When the alpha-2 receptors are antagonized the brain naturally produces more norepinephrine within the brain.

Concentration Curve: Yohimbine is characterized by quick absorption and a short elimination half-life. It reaches its peak plasma level just 1 hour after you take it and is practically out of system after only 5 hours.

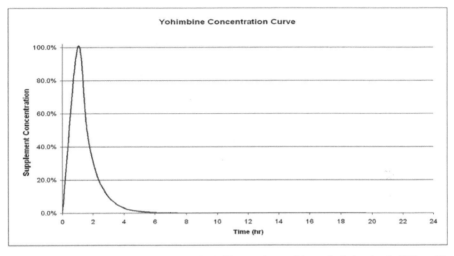

Concentration curve for Yohimbine with Peak Plasma time = 1 hr and elimination half-life = 40 minutes

Effect on Dreams: Yohimbine has a profound effect on dreaming. Dream vividness and memory are perhaps even better than with the acetylcholine boosting supplements. However sleep is possible only with very small doses. The dreams I have had using Yohimbine have, for the most part, been very pleasing although I have felt some anxiety during the dreams if the dose is greater than about 1 mg. There is one subtle point that I have noticed with Yohimbine: it does not seem to initiate REM sleep, but rather must work in conjunction with it. During normal REM sleep the norepinephrine system essentially shuts off and having elevated norepinephrine levels does little to push you into a dream state. However, if you are naturally entering a dream state the dreams become much more vivid and strong if norepinephrine levels are increased. This implies that

Yohimbine is much more effective when taken in the early morning hours when much more time is spent naturally in REM sleep.

Effect on Lucid Dreams: I consider Yohimbine to be one of the most powerful supplements available for lucid dream development. Yohimbine can be used as a lucid dream trigger if taken under the right conditions and acts much the same way as Galantamine in this respect. The downside of using Yohimbine as a trigger, is that you must be naturally entering REM sleep very soon after you take it. Also the doses that work best as triggers are incredibly close to the dose that will cause insomnia. For these reasons, I commonly use Galantamine as the main trigger and much smaller doses of Yohimbine as a complimentary substance. When used in this way the results are remarkable. Galantamine initiates REM sleep which initiates the effects of the Yohimbine. Once lucid the norepinephrine improves attention, focus, and working memory (a type of short term memory) far more than with Galantamine alone. These characteristics significantly boost the ability to reason within the dream. The mind stays clearer and does not get as easily distracted. This allows one to go deeper into the dream world in order to search for hidden potential and knowledge. It also improves the connection between the dream memory and the physical memory. Within the dream, memories can be recalled and even relived much easier than without it. This improved connection also helps to ensure that you carry out your entire set of dream experiments while within the dream.

Side Effects: At the doses I recommend side effects are extremely rare, but keep in mind that everyone is different. If overflow should occur (a sign you need to reduce the dose) you may feel hot, experience increased heart rate and pressure, feel a nervous ache in your joints as well as experience sweaty palms and feet. In more extreme cases anxiety, tremors, dizziness, and vomiting may be experienced. Yohimbine may trigger anxiety or panic attacks in prone individuals. An overdose of Yohimbine may be deadly – watch out for salivation, enlarged pupils, irregular heartbeat, and low blood pressure. An overdose needs to be treated immediately by emergency medical professionals.

Dosage: I consider the 9mg dose of Yohimbine that is typically included in a single capsule as insanely high. The first dose I took was 3 mg and I experienced significant overflow. For me, overflow typically stops at about 1.5 mg however it is literally impossible to fall to sleep on this high of dose. At about 0.75 – 1 mg, Yohimbine can be used as a lucid dream trigger. To use Yohimbine synergistically with Galantamine, I typically use 0.35 – 0.5 mg. Using a 0.35 dose implies that you divide a single 9 mg tablet into ~ 25 pieces.

Special Notes: Yohimbine is available as an over the counter the supplement. It is sold either as pure Yohimbe Bark or as a more concentrated form that is either standardized to 2%, 4%, or 8% Yohimbine. Remember that it is the Yohimbine that boosts norepinephrine. All of the standardized forms usually contain 9 mg of Yohimbine per tablet. I don't recommend buying the pure Yohimbe Bark because you don't know exactly how much Yohimbine is in each capsule and in fact it can vary greatly from capsule to capsule. I prefer the 8% Yohimbine form because it comes in a solid tablet instead of a powder filled capsule. This makes it easier to cut it into smaller pieces using a razor blade rather than trying to divide up a powder.

Summary: Yohimbine is an alpha-2 adrenergic antagonist which means that it can boost norepinephrine levels in the brain. Typical doses are 20 – 25 times too strong for the lucid dream enthusiast which will require dividing up the tablet into much smaller pieces. Yohimbine can act as lucid dream trigger around a dose of 1 mg but this borderlines on a dose that can cause insomnia. Using 0.5 mg or less simultaneously with Galantamine can produce extremely high level lucid dreams. This combination seems to work better than all others when the goal is a search for knowledge within the dream. This combination also seems to make your physical memories more accessible within the dream.

Yohimbine Summary Table	
Mechanism of action	Alpha-2 adrenergic antagonist which causes norepinephrine to produced within the brain
Able to cross the blood brain barrier	Yes
Time to peak plasma levels	1 hours
Elimination half-life	40 minutes
Maximum daily dose	9 mg (way way too high for lucid dreaming)
Lucid dream dose	0.75 - 1 mg when used as a trigger. 0.35-0.5 mg when used in combination with Galantamine
Effect on dreams	Extremely vivid senses and excellent recall
Effect on Lucid dreams	Greatly improves the ability to reason during a lucid dream. Improves memory of physical life

13

5-HTP (5-hydroxytryptophan)

General Description: 5-hydroxytryptophan (5-HTP) is the immediate precursor of serotonin and while serotonin does not cross the blood brain barrier, 5-HTP does. Due to its ability to increase serotonin levels within the brain, 5-HTP has been used for a variety of therapeutic purposes that include combating depression, reducing stress and anxiety, promoting sleep, and fighting off certain types of migraine headaches. It has also been used to suppress appetites. In general, the reports surrounding 5-HTP are positive but keep in mind that 5-HTP has only been available in the US since for a short time (since 1994) although it has been used in Europe for decades.

Concerning lucid dream development, 5-HTP plays an important yet indirect role. As I will point out in part three, 5-HTP and Melatonin both play a unique role. Using 5-HTP correctly will accomplish the following:

1. Improve the overall quality of sleep on the nights that you attempt to achieve high level lucid dreams.
2. Increase chance of success of having a lucid dream by taking advantage of the REM rebound effect.
3. Increase the length of a lucid dream by taking advantage of the REM rebound effect.

4. Increase ability to fall to sleep after taking more stimulating substances such as Galantamine or Yohimbine (see part 3 for details).

Mechanism of Action: 5-HTP is the immediate precursor to serotonin. 5-HTP supplements results in increase levels of serotonin in the brain by making available the required chemicals to produce serotonin.

Concentration Curve: 5-htp is characterized by quick absorption and a short elimination half-life. These properties make it ideal to take just before going to sleep. It reaches its peak plasma levels just 90 minutes after you take it and has reduced to just about 12% concentration after 6 hours of sleep (~4 sleep cycles).

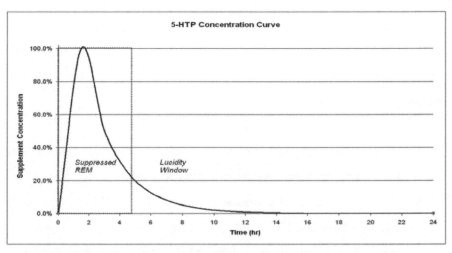

Concentration curve for 5-HTP with Peak Plasma time = 1.5 hr and elimination half-life = 1.5 hr

Effect on Dreams: 5-HTP has a positive effect on dream length and quality. Dream enhancement due to 5-HTP is most likely due to REM suppression followed by REM rebound and this results in increased dream vividness in the morning hours as the substance is wearing off. 5-HTP quickly increases serotonin levels that bring on deep and restful sleep. Due to the short half-life however, the 5-HTP is practically out of your system after 5 or 6 hours (assuming you don't take a large dose). This results in increased REM time in the early morning hours which produces more vivid dreams. Furthermore, I have found that the dream vividness, especially the visual aspect, is extremely clear. I have also found that when taking 5-HTP by itself, I am prone to experience calm and refreshing dreams. Although the dream vividness is high, my dream recall is a bit fuzzy. Sometimes I find that I act more like an observer than an active participant in dreams that are brought about by 5-HTP.

Effect on Lucid Dreams: 5-HTP plays a supporting role in lucid dream development. The main reason I use 5-HTP is to increase my overall quality of sleep on nights that I attempt to have lucid dreams. I accomplish this by taking 100-150 mg of 5-HTP just before bedtime. This increases my serotonin levels and helps to have more time spent in the deep non-REM sleep stages during the first half of the night. When I wake up after 4 or 5 hours I am almost always dreaming. I then take the supplements that trigger lucid dreaming and go back to bed. After several hours of intense lucid dreams I climb out of bed and feel refreshed and rejuvenated.

<u>Side Effects:</u> The most common side effects of 5-HTP are nausea and gastrointestinal distress. The nausea problem can be resolved by starting at a low dose and then gradually increasing it. Even when large doses are taken the problem tends to diminish over time. Personally I have never experienced any negative side effects with 5-HTP. I typically use 100 – 150 mg taken at or just before bedtime.

5-HTP should not be taken with prescription anti-depressants (this includes St. John's Wort) without the direct consultation of a doctor. Many of these anti-depressants act by also increasing serotonin levels and therefore could magnify the effects and possibly lead to potentially dangerous condition known as Serotonin Syndrome. Due to the short time this supplement has been available there are not a lot of studies that have investigated the long term effects of taking 5-HTP.

<u>Dosage:</u> There is no maximum recommended dose associated with 5-HTP. However, a reasonable dose range is probably between 50 and 300 mg. For treating depression doses up to 500 mg daily are used. At the lower doses side affects are rare.

<u>Special Notes:</u> You should not take vitamin B6 with 5-HTP as it may catalyze the reaction to serotonin in the gut rather than in the brain. Remember that serotonin does not pass through the blood brain barrier and so you want to keep the 5-HTP intact until the barrier has been crossed. There is some speculation (although no clinical research that I could find) that theorizes building up serotonin in the blood rather than in the brain could cause heart damage. This theory has not been confirmed or denied but should not be an issue unless

you are taking large amounts of vitamin B6 simultaneously with 5-HTP.

Summary: 5-HTP is the immediate precursor to serotonin. Increased serotonin levels lead to a state of calm relaxation and have been shown clinically to suppress REM sleep by favoring the deeper, non-REM stages. Since 5-HTP has a short elimination half life, it can be taken just before bedtime for the purpose of suppressing REM sleep and increasing the time spent in non-REM sleep. As the dose wears off, REM rebound occurs and is usually accompanied by more vivid dream experiences. If a lucid dream trigger (such as Galantamine) is taken at this time, there is an increase in odds of becoming lucid. Also, since lucid dream triggers usually suppress non-REM sleep in favor of REM sleep, 5-HTP can act to balance the amount of time spent in each phase during the night which results in a more balanced night's sleep. By maintaining balanced sleep practices you will not feel energy deprived following a lucid dream attempt and can increase the frequency of lucid dream attempts.

5-HTP Summary Table	
Mechanism of action	Direct precursor to serotonin
Able to cross the blood brain barrier	Yes
Time to peak plasma levels	1.5 hours
Elimination half-life	1.5 hours
Maximum daily dose	Up to 500 mg used to treat depression
Lucid dream dose	100-150 mg taken at bedtime
Effect on dreams	Increased vividness in second half of night
Effect on Lucid dreams	Increases odds of becoming lucid when used prior to Galantamine. Increases overall sleep quality by suppressing REM in first half of the night

14

Melatonin

General Description: Melatonin is a hormone that is released from the pineal gland and is thought to help us fall to sleep. Since Melatonin production is enhanced in darkness and decreased by light exposure it is often said that Melatonin has some control over our circadian rhythm and has the ability to reset our internal clocks. For this reason, Melatonin is sometimes used to reduce jet lag. Although Melatonin is synthesized from serotonin and 5-HTP is synthesized to serotonin, they both have a similar effect on sleep: both can help you fall to sleep and both can cause vivid dreams as the doses are wearing off. For this reason Melatonin is a possible alternative to 5-HTP although I tend to use it for a different purpose.

There are three characteristics that make Melatonin my second choice for suppressing REM. First of all Melatonin has an extremely short half-life. Since melatonin's half-life is only 40 minutes, one has to take a pretty large dose to suppress REM for 4 or 5 hours. I estimate that 3 mg would be necessary to suppress REM for four hours. Secondly, I find it difficult to fall to back to sleep after the Melatonin has worn off. Thirdly, I experience more vivid dreams using 5-HTP than I do using Melatonin.

There is however another way to use Melatonin that may be advantages to some. Research has shown that only 0.3 mg of Melatonin is necessary to induce sleep.

At this low dose, REM sleep is not suppressed and therefore Melatonin can be used simultaneously with Galantamine (or other supplements) if falling back to sleep is a problem. When I used Yohimbine as the lucidity trigger I would often use very small doses of Melatonin to aid in falling to sleep. This proved to be a fairly successful method. The time it took to fall to sleep was decreased by about half and furthermore, I was much more relaxed while awake and waiting for sleep onset. For this to work, it is important to keep the dose low, as I did notice a reduced chance in becoming lucid even at 0.5 mg of Melatonin.

Mechanism of Action: Serotonin is the precursor to Melatonin therefore Melatonin supplements probably don't do much to serotonin levels. However, Melatonin can help to fall asleep and suppress REM sleep.

Concentration Curve: Melatonin is characterized by quick absorption and a short elimination half-life. It reaches its peak plasma level just 60 minutes after you take it and is essentially out of your system after 6 hours (~4 sleep cycles).

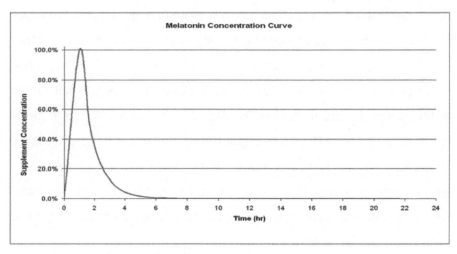

Concentration curve for Melatonin with Peak Plasma time=1hr and elimination half-life=40min

Effect on Dreams: Melatonin has been shown clinically to increase the time spent in REM sleep in the morning hours (as the dose is wearing off). It is theorized that this phenomena is due to a REM rebound effect. I have found 5-HTP to produce more vivid dreams than Melatonin but there are plenty of people who have commented on increased dream vividness and duration by using Melatonin. As with 5-HTP I find it more difficult to remember the details of the dream than I do when using the acetylcholine or norepinephrine boosting supplements.

Effect on Lucid Dreams: I use Melatonin as supporting supplement. When I am taking a lucid dream mix that I know causes insomnia, I will sometimes add 0.3 mg of Melatonin to help me fall asleep. At this small dose, REM is not suppressed and one can maintain excellent odds of becoming lucid.

Side Effects: There are no known serious side effects of using Melatonin supplements although long term side effects have not been studied. Some people who have taken Melatonin have reported sleepiness, headache, a "heavy-head" feeling, stomach discomfort, depression or feeling hungover. There are animal studies that suggest that large doses of Melatonin can interfere with fertility.

Dosage: When using Melatonin, less is better in my opinion. There are tablets available in 1, 2, 3 and 5 mg doses. There is no maximum daily dose suggested although the long terms effects of Melatonin are largely unknown. My typical dose is ~0.33mg (a 1mg tablet cut into three pieces). I do not however, use Melatonin on any kind of regular basis.

Summary: Melatonin is a hormone that is formed from serotonin. It has the potential to suppress REM sleep and can be used as a sleep aid. I find that 5-HTP is superior to Melatonin for the purpose of producing vivid dream experiences and I find it difficult to fall back to sleep after the Melatonin has worn off. My preferred way to use Melatonin is in very small doses (<0.5 mg) as an aid to fall to back to sleep after taking some of the more stimulating lucid dream supplements.

Melatonin Summary Table	
Mechanism of action	Substance that serotonin is synthesized into.
Able to cross the blood brain barrier	Yes
Time to peak plasma levels	1 hours
Elimination half-life	40 minutes
Maximum daily dose	up to 3 mg daily
Lucid dream dose	Up to 3 mg if using to suppress REM. Less than 0.5 mg if using as a sleep aid with other supplements
Effect on dreams	Can increases dream vividness due to REM rebound
Effect on Lucid dreams	Insignificant, but can help to fall to sleep when using more stimulating supplements

Part 3:

Achieving High Level Lucid Dreams

15

Are You Ready For This?

I remember the first day I went parachuting like it was yesterday. I arrived at the drop zone at 7:30 AM with a stomach full of butterflies. "Can I do this?" I wondered. My mind was full of excitement, anticipation, doubt, and fear. I then proceeded to go through a detailed four hour long class that went repeatedly over exactly what to do in every possible situation. Time and time again I went through the exact details of how to climb out of the plane and hang from the wing, how to arch my back and let go, how to stay mentally alert while falling, how to handle any one of dozens of potential problems that might occur, how to steer my chute and keep my bearings, and finally how land so that I didn't get hurt. At the end of the class the instructor came around to each one of us and asked, "Are you ready for this?" I answered with a confident "Yes". I felt ready, really ready.

But then it happened, I put on my parachute, walked out into the middle of a large grassy field and climbed into the small Cessna. My first impression of the plane was that of an old VW Beetle with wings and then after the engine started I revised my impression to be that of an old VW Beetle with wings that needed a tune-up. My stomach started to ache and my muscles and joints felt weak and uncomfortable. We took off and proceeded to fly in circles around the drop zone.

I looked nervously out of the window and watched as each circle took us higher and higher. The jump altitude was ~3500 ft and suddenly the engines quieted and pilot/jump master opened his window to let in a blast of wind and then motioned for me to move forward to the door. To say that I was overflowing with fear is a bit of an understatement but I managed to keep myself together and crawl to the door. "Open the door" shouted the jump master. I turned the knob and the door flew open with a mighty thrush. The jump master locked the door in place and then bellowed the next command, "Position!" he shouted. In hindsight, I now understand that I was in partial shock and my fear had turned to total numbness as I placed my foot out on the 3 inch by 10 inch step protruding from the side of the plane. My foot was followed by my hand that grabbed onto the strut connecting the wing to the plane. The view was amazing but I couldn't enjoy it. I had always considered myself to be scared of heights, but I was so high that it didn't even seem to be real and all I felt was numbness. Then my second hand followed. I slide both hands out along the strut as I stepped fully out of the plane. The wind noise and pressure were intense. Then I let my feet hang out in the open air behind me. It's much easier to hang from the wing of a plane than you might think, if for no other reason than the death grip that you impose on the strut. I looked in the plane knowing that there was no turning back.

The jump master looked me in the eye and gave the thumbs up. With that signal I turned my head forward and looked up at a small red dot painted on the underside of the wing and let go. The next several seconds are a total blur of which I only remember a vivid sight of the plane rapidly diminishing in size followed by a series of jerks. "I'm alive!" I almost cried. Then I heard a voice coming from the radio I was wearing around my neck. "Yah hoo! Nice jump. Your lines are a bit twisted so your going to have to kick yourself out" the voice said. "What?" I looked up, "Oh my God!" The series of lines that connected my harness to the parachute were twisted around each other keeping the slider, a small piece of fabric that locks the chute open, from sliding into place. I was almost panicking as the thoughts raced through my head "What do I do, what do I do?" As if on cue the voice in radio said again, "You're going to have to kick yourself out". The memory came back and I proceeded to kick my legs out in a big circular motion. This got me spinning around and around until the cords fully untwisted and the slider slide into place. I breathed the biggest sigh of relief that is possible for a living being. For the first time I really looked down. There I was suspended about 2500 feet above the ground. The only sound was that of the wind. The farms below looked only like rectangles of various sizes and shades of green. The trees reminded me of tiny pieces of broccoli spread across a plate. "Reach up and release your brakes" shouted the voice in the radio. I looked up and could see the two steering ropes that were Velcro'd into the slow brake position. The handles were about 15" above the white knuckle grip that I was using to hold onto the main lines. I suddenly realized that the only thing really holding me in the harness were two nylon strips that wrapped around my legs. "If those break I'm going to fall right out of this chute", I thought and once again I was overcome by fear. I looked up again, "Calm down". I reached up with one hand and released the brake followed by the other. At this point I could begin to steer the chute and my stress finally started to transform into pure and intense enjoyment. I let out a series of yah hoos that were so loud that they could be clearly heard on the ground (or so I was told). I glided down, performing a series of circles, both very large and some very tight until I dropped gently on the ground. Alright maybe it wasn't so gentle but I had done it and lived to talk about it.

The point of this story is to understand that no amount of intellectual or technical training could have prepared me for the real experience of jumping out of an airplane. The same is true of lucid dreaming, in general, and especially for the supplement approach to lucid dreaming. There are two types of lucid dreams that are popularly recognized: DILDs and WILDs. DILD refers to a lucid dream that starts as a normal (non-lucid) dream. In this case the dreamer typically recognizes that "something isn't quite right" and then suddenly becomes aware that they are dreaming. It has been reported that ~90% of all lucid dreams are DILDs and only 10% are WILDs. Using the supplement approach I find the opposite to be true; well over 90% are WILDs. WILD refers to a phenomenon of moving directly from waking consciousness into a dream with total continuity. The actual transition from the physical world to the dream world can be every bit as intense as jumping out of an airplane. For this reason I can say with confidence that I can not fully prepare you for the experience. I can only let you know about my experiences, what might occur to you, and to let you know that others have gone before and crossed between worlds and lived to talk about.

Typical Experiences: The following paragraphs summarize the four types of transitions that make up the majority of my supplement induced WILDs. I have listed them in order from the most gentle to the most intense.

1. The most gentle transitions are the ones in which the dream world comes to me rather than me going to the dream world. Images start forming in the mind and become increasingly detailed and complex. Suddenly there is a fully detailed dream environment that fills my mind. At this point, I am only an observer and am not fully integrated into either the plot or the fabric of the dream. The actual transition can be swift and surprising. The dream seems to wrap around you and you suddenly find yourself standing in a fully animated dream world. As an example consider the following experience that occurred to me. I was lying on my right side with eyes closed and waiting patiently for my lucid dream to start. Images of varying detail were floating in and out of my awareness. An image formed that started as dark impressions lacking in shape and detail. Colors started to become richer and the images began to take on familiar and recognizable shapes. The images started as discrete and separated, but then started to form a single complex view. It was a room. I watched objects come into focus: a bed, a bookshelf filled with books, toys scattered on the floor. Then another form started to appear. The form transitioned from a slew of colors into a boy about seven years old standing in front of me. The details became increasingly clearer. The boy came into perfect focus. Stripped shirt, brown hair and pale complexion are just a few of the details. Suddenly the boy turned his head

and looked me directly in my minds eye as though fully aware I was there. His look was so piercing that it surprised me and I backed up. Then I noticed that I had really backed up! It was at this point that I became aware of my dream body and found myself standing in the room facing the child. From there the lucid experience began. This type of transitioning experience accounts for about 10% of my WILDs.

2. More often the dream does not come to the dreamer but the dreamer must go to the dream. This is much more profound. The most gentle of these types of transitions generally starts as a feeling of floating, or at least as certain parts of your body as floating, which are distinct and separate from the physical body. After a little practice with this feeling you learn that your mind has in fact already formed your dream body and it is lying in a more or less coincident position with your physical body. Your awareness has already started to shift to the dream world but has done so tactilely rather than visually. In these cases it is possible to guide your dream body away from your physical body and then you just need to stand up and walk away. Now comes the debate about out of body experiences and lucid dreams. Typically when I get up and walk away I am in my bedroom. I can walk around the house as I please until my surroundings transform into a different locale either naturally or by a conscious effort. Was I walking around my physical house or a dream representation of my physical house? Although I can't say with 100% certainty, I believe the latter. I believe that it is very natural for the mind

to create a dream representation of the place that you physically laid down under this set of circumstances. Your consciousness remained unbroken during the transition. Your consciousness remembers coming in and lying down on your bed. So it is natural that your consciousness believes you are still there once you enter the dream. In lucid dreaming it's all about belief. If you really believe it, it is real within a lucid dream. Since my consciousness is continuous and because I am certain I laid down on my bed, when I stand up and walk away I must be walking away from my bed. If you follow the program outlined in this book you can decide for yourself because you will undoubtedly experience this phenomenon. This type of experience accounts for about 40% of my WILDS.

3. The third type of transition is quite common and can be very intense. Once again consciousness remains unbroken but this time I experience what I refer to as intense accelerations as a means of moving into the dream world. This is almost always just a tactile sensation that involves my body suddenly accelerating in a particular direction at incredible speeds. The velocity can vary greatly from experience to experience but can be faster and more realistic than you can possibly imagine. Furthermore I may suddenly stop or change direction in a totally unpredictable way. In the beginning you will probably have no control over this but after a while you can influence it a bit. Once the shock factor of this event has worn off you will most likely really enjoy the experience (at

least I do) but the first few times might really freak you out. Don't let it scare you, it is natural and it happens all of the time. Now when I feel the accelerations starting I get a smile on my dream body's face and try to prolong the experience by pushing myself to faster and faster speeds. Sometime I feel a texture underneath me, like I am being dragged across the ground (don't worry it never hurts). There is also a less common, but thoroughly enjoyable, type of acceleration that has occurred as I was trying to roll out of my physical body just as the accelerations started. The result was a spin that the Tasmania devil would have been proud of. Generally when the acceleration stops I either find myself in a dream or in my bedroom in which I just get up and walk away. This type of experience accounts for about 45% of my WILDs.

4. The last type of transition has only occurred to me twice and therefore is very rare. It involves a sense of vibration that starts at the back of my head and spine and grows incredibly intense as it moves towards the front of my head. It's like walking backwards through an electric curtain. There are no words that can explain the intensity of the experience. Both times were accompanied by a sense of paralysis and although the sensation only lasted for about 20 seconds it is life changing. The sensations start mild and then grow more intense in an exponential manner until your very soul is being shaken loose from the physical world. Then, in an instant, the sensation totally vanishes. At this point you are free to get up and walk into the dream world.

It would be foolish to think that these are the only types of transitions that occur; they are merely the only ones I have personally experienced. It would be equally foolish for you to think that an intellectual account of these experiences can come close to capturing the real experience of these transitions. They are all life changing. Advanced lucid dreaming is not for the meek and timid, you are moving into a virtually unknown dimension that is every bit as real as the physical. Although you shouldn't be scared of the unknown, you should always maintain the very deepest respect for it.

16

Understanding the Strategy

Using supplements to achieve high level lucid dreaming requires a strategy if one wants to maximize the odds of becoming lucid while also maximizing the frequency of attempts. The strategy that I have developed is simple and effective. In the most general sense the strategy can be broken down into four elements:

- Place health and well being first.
- Maintain high quality and balanced sleep.
- Achieve high level lucid dreams.
- Counteract the effects of desensitization and tolerance.

Let's take a deeper look at each one of these elements.

Place health and well being first: I follow a couple of rules that I never compromise when it comes to health and supplements.

1. Always start with a small dose and then increase it only to the point of effectiveness.
2. Never exceed the maximum recommended daily dose (as set by clinical research).

3. Always take supplements individually first before combining them with other supplements.

4. Always track and record any side effects no matter how small they may be, remembering that side effects can be physical, mental, and/or emotional.

<u>Maintain high quality and balanced sleep:</u> Sleep is too often an afterthought in our lives yet is has a profound effect on our quality of life. I am a father, a husband, a full time employee, a writer, a homeowner, a lucid dreamer, and much more. At times trying to manage everything seems both impossible and impractical. Even with a busy schedule however, I do not sacrifice my sleep, nor do I sleep my life away. I strive for 7-8 hours of sleep at least five nights a week and I try to never drop below six hours. More sleep isn't needed but less sleep in detrimental to our physical, mental and emotional health. For healthy dreaming, you need 7-8 hours of sleep per night.

This will not only improve your state mind but also greatly improve your odds of becoming lucid. Achieving frequent, high level lucid dreams will demand some shifts in the way you sleep. Here are some simple rules to follow that have proven to work extremely well.

1. Always sleep 4-5 hours before attempting to have a lucid dream

2. Do not attempt lucid dreams on nights that you feel physically, mentally, or emotionally exhausted.

3. If attempting three of more nights of lucid dreaming per week, actively suppress REM sleep in the hours before each attempt.

Quality sleep is probably the most often overlooked, yet extremely important aspect of lucid dream practice. Sleep research has shown that when we first fall to sleep after an active day, we naturally and quickly drop into deep non-REM sleep. There are few, if any, well documented reports of lucid dreams occurring during the deep sleep stages. Also keep in mind that supplements which act as lucid dream triggers do not let you go into the deep stages of sleep; this is one of the reasons why they work so well. Taking acetylcholine boosting supplements or norepinephrine boosting supplements at the beginning of night is not practical nor an effective means of inducing lucid dreams. When this is done the body is placed in a state of conflict; the body wants deep sleep but the supplements won't allow it. The result is no lucid dream AND poor quality of sleep.

Remember that deep sleep is associated with elevated serotonin levels and low acetylcholine and norepinephrine levels. By allowing yourself to sleep four or five hours before taking a lucid dream trigger, you are allowing your body to complete about three full sleep cycles. This is the turning point where the body starts to favor the REM sleep stage instead of the deep sleep stages in natural sleep. When a trigger is taken at this time it works more synergistically with the body instead of putting the body in a state of conflict. There is some time spent in deep non-REM sleep during the second half of the night, and taking these supplements will suppress it well beyond what is natural. For this reason, one might feel somewhat energy deprived following a night of supplement induced lucid dreaming. This can be almost totally avoided if REM is suppressed in the first half of the night. For example, if a modest dose of 5-HTP is taken just before bedtime, the serotonin levels in the brain will be elevated. The dose works synergistically with the brain because it wants deep sleep in the first half of the night and increased serotonin levels are associated with deep sleep. Whereas the brain naturally has some short periods of REM sleep, the 5-HTP will act to suppress them by continuously crossing the blood brain barrier and converting into serotonin, therefore maintaining a more or less constant deep sleep. As the 5-HTP wears off, the brain will want to make up for the lost time spent in REM and will suppress some of the non-REM sleep in the early morning hours. If a lucid dream trigger is taken at this transition point, the result will be more or less a split yet balanced night's sleep: deep non-REM sleep in the first half of the night and REM (lucid dream) sleep in the second half. Not only does this result in a restful night's sleep but it can also noticeably extend the length of your lucid dreams.

Finally don't forego your common sense in the search of lucid dreams. If you are physically, mentally or emotionally exhausted, take the night off and get some rest. The same is true if you are ill. In these cases your body will require more deep sleep than usual and you should let your body heal itself.

Achieve high level lucid dreams: There are more elements involved in achieving a high level lucid dream than just taking a supplement. So much so that I have dedicated an entire part of this book to the subject (see Part 4: Increasing Your Odds). The most important element, without a doubt, is to have the right state of mind. Although it is true that you have to want it to happen in order to have any chance of success, you must expect it to happen if you want to get your success rate up above 90%. One of the main reasons my success is so extremely high is that I know that I will have a lucid dream on the nights I try to do so. Of course one of the reasons I am so sure is that I've had many successful attempts on which to build my confidence.

The next important element is to take the right combination of supplements at the right time. If you follow the program outlined in the next few chapters, you will quickly find what works for you and what doesn't.

The third element is patience. In a high level lucid dream you are neither fully asleep nor are you fully awake; or to put it another way, you are simultaneously asleep and awake. The lucid state is a borderline state located between the classical definition of sleep and wakefulness. Therefore the triggers that work best do not lend themselves to easily falling to sleep, nor should they. An important key to success is to lie quietly and just be patient. There is no rush. Have faith that the dreams will come. This takes a bit of getting use to. Don't talk to yourself. Don't analyze the situation. Don't keep flip flopping positions. Remain relaxed and lie there patiently. I have developed a few exercises designed to move someone from wakefulness into the lucid state. These exercises have made a big impact on my success rate and will be explained in Part 4 of this book.

Finally there is an art to making the actual transition into the dream. The experience of transitioning from the physical into the dream is awe inspiring and life changing. In the beginning you may have nights where you go right to the edge but just miss the transition. Usually this happens because you get too excited and wake yourself up. Don't let it frustrate you. It gets much easier after a few successes are behind you. After some practice you will find that you can bring yourself out of a lucid dream and then go back in many times during a single night.

Counteract the effects of desensitization and tolerance: The goal is not just to have one or two lucid dreams, it's to have high level lucid dreams frequently and for years to come. Desensitization and tolerance are very real phenomena and should not be underestimated. Fortunately there are a few techniques that work extremely well and should be incorporated right from the beginning. I will explain these techniques in detail in chapter 18, but the philosophy can be summarized as:

- Don't take a larger dose than necessary to get the result.
- Always let the supplements clear out of your system.
- If the supplements stay in your system well beyond the time of the lucid dream, actively counteract their effects if possible.
- Don't take the same combination twice in a row (i.e. alternate between several combinations).
- If necessary take some time off.

Following this simple philosophy I am able to have high level lucid dreams on an every other night basis with practically guaranteed success.

17

Primary Trigger Combination

I have listed eight different supplements that I have used with success in my own personal lucid dream development. So where should you start your own lucid dream development? The best way to induce a lucid dream using supplements is to use one of the proven lucid dream triggers. Recall that the triggers do more than just increase dream vividness and recall; they actually promote lucid dreaming. Lucid dream triggers work by allowing you to move from the waking state directly into the dream state (WILD) or by promoting enhanced reasoning skills that allow you to recognize your dream signs (DILD). In part 2, four lucid dream triggers were identified: Galantamine, GPC, Nicotine, and Yohimbine. Yohimbine increases norepinephrine levels and the other three increase acetylcholine levels. Here is my advice:

Don't start with Yohimbine: Yohimbine is proving to be one the most advanced supplements in my own development but it not the best starting place. Although I have found Yohimbine to be a successful trigger, it is more difficult to use than the others. Yohimbine does not initiate REM sleep and therefore requires that you naturally enter REM sleep shortly after taking it. This requires that you have a good understanding of your sleep cycle in order to use it effectively. The other disadvantage with Yohimbine is that there is a fine line between a successful lucid dream and insomnia.

To complicate the issue, your emotional state can noticeably affect the optimum dosage. If you feel any excitement or anticipation during an attempt your brain will naturally produce more norepinephrine. You may find that the same dose that worked on one night leads to insomnia on the next. For these reasons I don't recommend using Yohimbine as the primary trigger.

Don't start with Nicotine: I rarely use nicotine these days but I have had very good success with it. One could easily use Nicotine as a starting point for lucid dream development. Of all the supplements discussed, Nicotine has the most noticeable side effects. It has been shown to rapidly cause short term desensitization of the nicotinic ACh receptors and can eventually lead to long term (i.e. permanent) desensitization. These receptors are crucial for lucid dreaming so best not to desensitize them.

This leaves Galantamine and GPC. Remember that Galantamine inhibits the breakdown of ACh and GPC is a precursor to ACh. The two work very well together (as I will discuss in chapter 19). I recommend starting with Galantamine based on the fact that it is incredibly effective and because I have much more experience using it than I do with GPC. GPC has the advantage of being extremely well tolerated but it has the disadvantage of a longer time until peak plasma levels are reached; you may fall to sleep too early. If this should happen you will need to become lucid from within the dream (i.e. DILD) instead of moving directly from wakefulness into the dream (i.e. WILD).

<u>Start with Galantamine:</u> The very first night I tried Galantamine, I had a lucid dream that was almost an hour long. It is an extremely effective trigger. Galantamine is most effective if a Choline supplement is used in combination with it. Recall from chapters 7 & 8 that when Choline is combined with Galantamine, ACh levels rise more quickly, increasing your odds of moving directly into REM (dream) sleep. The type of Choline should be either Choline Bitartrate or Choline Citrate and can be purchased either premixed with Galantamine or as a separate supplement. Don't buy Galantamine that is part of a memory mix or that has Melatonin mixed in; you will just be confusing the issue. I recommend a dose of 4-8 mg of Galantamine combined with 250-500 mg of Choline. I recommend against higher doses of Galantamine because the risk of side effects come into play around the 12-16 mg level. I use the Galantamine/Choline mix as the primary trigger combination on which all other combinations are built.

<u>Procedure for inducing your first supplement based lucid dream:</u> Suggestions on how to have a successful lucid dream using the Galantamine/Choline trigger.

1. Do not consume Alcohol on the evening prior to the attempt. A single glass of wine with dinner may be alright, but keep it to a minimum.
2. Go to bed around 10:30 PM.
3. Sleep peacefully until 3:30 AM and get up. It is better if you can wake yourself up naturally without the use of an alarm clock but if you must use one set the volume just loud enough to be effective.

4. Get up and go to the toilet then take 4-8mg of Galantamine and 250-500mg of Choline Bitartrate or Choline Citrate with a cup of water.

5. If you feel overly groggy, stretch a little (no more than about five minutes). Remember that you do not want to fall immediately back to sleep. You want to transition into sleep after the supplements have started working.

6. Lie back in bed. I recommend lying on your back with your hands by your side. Make sure you're comfortable.

7. When you first lie down go over your intentions three times. Tell yourself something like, "The next thing I will experience will be a dream. I will recognize the dream state and become lucid. While I am in the dream I will (fill in whatever you want to do here)" and so on.

8. After you go over this three times quiet the mind. Whenever you find that you are thinking to yourself just casually stop. Don't get frustrated if you find your internal voice keeps talking, just keep letting it go without paying much attention to it.

9. After about twenty minutes turn onto your side. The Tibetan dream yoga suggests that men should sleep on their right side and women should sleep on their left side. The Tibetan's believe that for men, lying on the right side slightly compresses the body's right side energy channel. This suppresses negative emotions and encourages wisdom prana (vital energy) to flow in the left channel. The opposite is true for women. Sleeping on my right side has proven very effective.

10. Now just calmly relax and be patient.

It very well may take you over an hour to fall to sleep the first few times you try this. This is due to the ACh levels building, combined with your own excitement (excitement increases norepinephrine levels). It does become easier after a few successful attempts. Just keep lying there calmly and patiently waiting for the dream to come. You may start to experience a gentle throbbing sensation in your head. Don't get too excited if this happens. Just relax and wait. Once you see images coming and going in your mind you will know you are getting close. Remain passive, relax and wait. The more you can control your excitement the better your chances are of success and the sooner the lucid dream will come. The images will start to become more frequent and more vivid. You may start to experience a vibration in your head and neck, or a feeling of floating. Don't get excited. Just relax and wait. At this point a transition will likely occur. Remember that the transitions can come in many forms. If the vibrations get very strong or if you suddenly experience an incredible sensation of acceleration, you are probably already in your dream body and can just get up and walk away. However, for the first few attempts you should not get up. Instead just keep lying there patiently. This will result in a dream forming with you inside it and fully aware.

After you have gone in and explored a bit, I suggest you consciously wake yourself up. This is as easy as just deciding to do so from within the dream. This will help keep the memories fresh and vivid. Then get up and write everything down.

Many people will be successful on their first attempt. If you're not, don't worry about it, you'll get the feel of it after a few attempts. Whether you're successful or not, wait at least four days before trying again. Time will work in your favor here. I strongly recommend not taking Galantamine on two consecutive nights because you are not giving it enough time to completely clear out of your system. This may cause tolerance issues in the future. Follow this routine until you have experienced at least five high level lucid dreams. At this point you are ready to advance to the multiple trigger combinations outlined in the following chapters.

First Lucid Dream Procedure	
Supplement	Galantamine/Choline
When to take supplement	After 4-5 hours of sleep
How much supplement to take	4-8 mg Galantamine; 250-500 mg of Choline
Suggested body position	Either on lying on back or lying on right side (women may want to lie on their left side)
Key factors	Quiet the mind (don't talk to yourself)
	Relax
	Passively watch any images that form in your mind
	Form an intent to have a lucid dream
	Be patient and passively wait
What to expect.	1 or more hours before sleep
	Possible gentle throbbing in head
	Possible vibrations in head
	Possible feeling of floating
	Possible sensation of sudden acceleration
	Lucid dream
When to try again	Wait 4 or more days before another attempt.
When to advance to the multiple trigger combinations	After at least 5 high level lucid dreams using this approach.

18

Counteracting Desensitization and Tolerance

Desensitization and tolerance, although related, do not mean the same thing. Whereas desensitization is mainly a physiological effect, tolerance involves psychological aspects coupled to both direct and indirect physiological effects. The net result is the same however: The supplements just don't work as well as they use to.

After experiencing at least five high level lucid dreams using the method outlined in the previous chapter you may have noticed two subtle but important changes. First, the gentle throbbing in your head probably isn't as strong as it was the first time you tried Galantamine. Second, you probably can fall to sleep much easier than you could after the first few attempts. Both of these events are related to tolerance. The throbbing seems to occur due to the rapidly increasing levels of acetylcholine inside your brain caused by Galantamine. After a few times, the body is more tolerant to this rapid fluctuation. The time it takes to go to sleep is more controlled by your reactions and expectations. Strong excitement and anticipation cause norepinephrine to be released in the brain at the same time that Galantamine is acting to increase ACh levels. This makes falling to sleep much more difficult than the Galantamine does on its own.

Also, since norepinephrine also can act as a lucid dream trigger (see Yohimbine), your own excitement can actually increase your odds of success and even make any transitioning sensations more intense than Galantamine will cause on its own. A little bit of tolerance is to be expected, is natural, and can be handled quite easily.

Desensitization, on the other hand, must be avoided. Desensitization is a physiological event. Galantamine causes increased levels of acetylcholine to be present in the brain for up to 48 hours after you take a dose. This increased concentration can literally cause the receptors that the acetylcholine binds with to start to lose their sensitivity. This means that in order to have the same physiological effect you will need to increase the acetylcholine levels even further (i.e. take a larger dose of Galantamine) in order to get the same effect as you had with the initial doses. The larger dose causes further desensitization and hence a vicious cycle continues until one reaches a high enough dose that negative side effects begin to surface. Fortunately clinical studies show that Galantamine does not cause long term desensitization. Short term desensitization can be countered by letting the level of acetylcholine within the brain return to its normal state for some period of time before taking another dose.

I have been successful in avoiding tolerance and desensitization by following a simple and effective strategy:

<u>Don't take a larger dose than necessary to get the result.</u> There is no point in taking excessive doses of any supplement. Going beyond the dose required to produce the desired effect will ultimately

lead to more rapid tolerance build up and desensitization. Although I often refer to specific doses that work well for me, keep in mind that I determined these doses by a rather rigorous trial and error period. During this period I took only one supplement per night at either 11 PM or at 4 AM in order to record the effects that it had on my dreams. I started at very low doses and often had to cut up a single pill in many small pieces to get to what I considered to be a suitable starting point. I then worked my way up to find the dose levels that started to have a profound effect on my dreams. Then when I started combining supplements I reduced the doses and started to again build up to see what worked. Although this was a painstaking exercise it yielded a wealth of information about how each of these supplements can be used to produce some amazing lucid dreams and also what dose levels work best for me. I wouldn't expect that my optimum dose is equal to your optimum dose. It is a good idea to start at the low end of the dose range that I have included in my recommendations, and probably an even better idea to cut those doses in half and build up from there in order to optimize your own dose levels. By keeping the dosages to a minimum, you are minimizing the swing in your brain's neurotransmitter levels. By keeping this swing to more of a tilt, you are ensuring that the entire system stays balanced and robust. Swinging too far can not only lead to physical side effects, but can also lead to mood swings or even scattered thoughts.

Always let supplements totally clear out of your system. By letting the supplements clear out of your system, you are allowing your body to return to its normal state and for all of the neurotransmitters to return to their normal levels within the brain. Returning to the normal state for some period of time is an excellent way to guard against short term desensitization and therefore ensure that the supplements keep working as they should. The question that must be asked is how long does the body need to stay in its natural state before the short term desensitization is diminished? This is complicated question that depends on many factors and really has no simple answer, but my approach has been to let the body remain in the normal state for at least as long as the supplement was in the body.

For the most part, all of the supplements contained in this book have sufficiently cleared out of the body after about twelve hours. By using the rule above, this would imply that these supplements could be taken on a daily basis: 12 hours in the body plus 12 hours out of the body. The major exception to this is Galantamine which takes about 48 hours to clear out of the body. This implies that Galantamine should not be taken more frequently than once every four days in order to avoid any short term desensitization problems.

<u>If the supplements stay in your system well beyond the time of the lucid dream, actively counteract their effects if possible.</u> The four day rule for Galantamine works very well for me and I have seen my success rate drop if I try to shorten the time between attempts. That is, until I actively started trying to counteract its effects as soon as my lucid dream ended. Piracetam is a very useful substance to help normalize the cholinergic system. There have been many studies that show Piracetam helps optimize the efficiency with which

acetylcholine is used up. Some of these studies indicate that Piracetam can counteract both short term and long term desensitization of the ACh receptors by counteracting the effects of the drugs that are causing the desensitization to occur. Galantamine causes acetylcholine levels to increase by blocking the substance that is responsible for breaking it down. Since Galantamine is in your system for up to forty-eight hours it is reasonable to believe that your acetylcholine levels are higher than normal for this period of time. Higher than normal acetylcholine levels lead to short term desensitization. Piracetam's function is not to break down acetylcholine like acetylcholinesterase does (recall that Galantamine inhibits acetylcholinesterase), but instead it is thought to use the acetylcholine to help form and maintain memories. By using up the extra acetylcholine that Galantamine produces, Piracetam helps maintain lower levels of acetylcholine than would be maintained under the influence of Galantamine alone. The Piracetam/Galantamine combination results in a more normal level of acetylcholine in the brain and therefore there is less of a chance for desensitization to occur. With less desensitization, Galantamine can be taken more often.

As I stated in chapter 10 however, Piracetam seems to effectively counteract Galantamine's potential to trigger a lucid dream. This last point is taken solely from my own experience but I have, on numerous occasions, tried to use Piracetam or the Piracetam/Galantamine combination to induce a lucid dream with no success. Furthermore it seems as though my dream recall is particularly bad if I have significant amounts of Piracetam in my system and so for this reason I recommend making sure that

Piracetam is cleared out of your system before attempting the next lucid dream.

There are a few key points to understand in order to understand how to use Piracetam to combat desensitization.

1. Although Piracetam is known to be extremely safe even at very large doses, it is important to ramp down a dose when using it if you plan to take more than 3000 mg in a single day. One of Piracetam's functions is to increase blood flow to the brain. This increased blood produces some of the benefits of using Piracetam but can lead to a headache if the Piracetam suddenly wears off and the blood flow becomes more constricted. This can be completely avoided if you spread out the dose of Piracetam throughout the day.

2. Piracetam has a relatively long half-life at five hours. This requires about 36 hours to completely clear out of the system.

3. The recommended daily dose of Piracetam is 2400-4800 mg. This dose range has been shown clinically to have the optimum effect on memory enhancement. Piracetam usually comes in 800 mg capsules so 3-6 capsules per day are recommended.

4. Piracetam should be taken immediately following a lucid dream attempt. This is the time when ACh levels are at their peak and therefore the most critical time to counter desensitization. I recommend taking 2400 mg of Piracetam as soon as you wake up from an attempt. I have experimented with 2400 mg/day and 4800 mg/day. Both dose levels seem equally effective and therefore I favor a single dose just after

awakening. If you plan on taking a higher dose you can add 800 mg approximately every five hours. This approach will allow blood concentrations to gradually decrease, avoiding a possible headache.

The following graph shows the overlap of a 4800 mg dose of Piracetam with a single dose of Galantamine. The Piracetam is spread throughout the day with 2400 mg taken upon awakening and then 800 mg taken every five hours thereafter. Notice that the overall concentration of Piracetam is gradually being reduced in the blood stream and that both supplements are completely cleared out of the body after 48 hours.

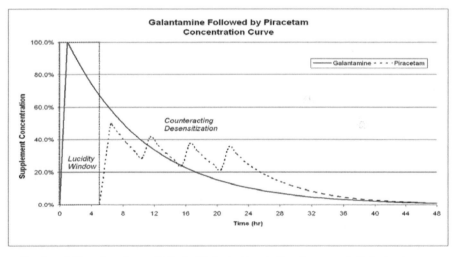

Overlap of Piracetam dose with that of Galantamine. In the above graph Galantamine was taken at 3 AM, 2400 mg of Piracetam was taking at 8 AM, 800 mg of Piracetam was taken each at 1 PM, 6 PM and 11 PM.

<u>Don't take the same combination twice in a row (i.e. alternate between several successful combinations).</u> If you take the exact same combination of supplements every time you try to have a lucid

dream your body starts to get use to it. This is a form of tolerance. The mind may become too lackadaisical and after some time you may notice the effectiveness starting to wane, especially if you are making attempts more than twice a week. The best method I have found to keep things fresh is to mix it up a bit. I regularly use Galantamine/Choline as the primary trigger combination however, on one night I might add some Mucuna Pruriens and then on the next attempt I may add some Yohimbine, maybe after that I try Galantamine/Choline by itself or with a little GPC. The point is that my body never quite knows what I am going to throw at it and this keeps things fresh. I also keep detailed records of each attempt so I can go back and see what combinations regularly produce the most astounding results. By mixing things up, the body never really adapts and my lucid dreams remain extremely strong.

Keep your expectations high. Don't underestimate the power of your mind. I remember the first very high level lucid dream I had. There were no supplements involved. I had maybe two dozen low to medium level lucid dream experiences that were spread out over several years of trying. On this particular night I took the trash outside and looked up at the sky. The sky was clear and the air was crisp. I could see Saturn and Jupiter defining the ecliptic that led to a moon that was about 90% full. In an instant I was positive that I was going to have a lucid dream that night. My certainty is difficult to explain but it was both sincere and total. When I laid down that night I felt at ease and relaxed. My lucid dream that night was immensely profound, long and marked by excellent dream manipulation skills. After that night I tried to recapture that certainty on many occasions but I only sincerely felt it every so often. Each time I did feel it however, I succeeded in having a lucid dream. Now with supplements, things are much easier but the role of the mind should not be neglected. You need to want it, not just a little bit, but with everything you have, as though your own future depended on becoming lucid that particular night. More than wanting it, you need to expect it; to be sure of it; to not settle for anything less. When you're having high level lucid dreams multiple times per week, there will be those times that your heart just isn't in it. You may be tired, or you may not have planned out anything special, or your mind may just be preoccupied with something else. In these cases, do yourself a favor and take the night off. Keep your mind focused on the goal of becoming lucid and your success rate will be much higher than if you just wake up at 4 AM to take a pill and then go back to sleep.

If necessary take some time off. For whatever reason sometimes the supplements just don't work. This could be from tolerance or desensitization or maybe just be due to something going on in your life. When this occurs you should take a couple extra days off before trying again. Two extra days seems to do a world of good. During the time off, focus on what it is you want to achieve during your next lucid dream and let your body just sleep naturally. Since I often experience intense accelerations when transitioning into a dream, I use this as a marker for effectiveness. If the accelerations seem less intense than usual I will usually take an extra day off before trying again. The same is true if my dream recall seems to be dropping off. To me this is a much better approach than to wait until I don't succeed in having a lucid dream at all. There is nothing wrong with taking a break from time to time. This will help keep the quality of the lucid experiences exceptionally high.

19

Multiple Trigger Combinations

Hopefully by now you have developed a first hand understanding of the power the Galantamine/Choline combination has as the primary lucid dream trigger. In this chapter we build upon that power to form four incredibly effective trigger combinations. The reason these combinations are so effective is they include more than one trigger. When multiple triggers are combined, the likelihood of experiencing a lucid dream is increased. In addition, dream length and mental clarity are both positively influenced.

In Part 2, I identified four supplements as lucid dream triggers: Galantamine, GPC, Nicotine, and Yohimbine. Each of the combinations in this chapter includes the primary trigger combination (Galantamine/Choline) and adds one or more of the other triggers in order to enhance the result.

The Primary Trigger:

As was pointed out in chapter 17, Galantamine and Choline combine to form the primary lucid dream trigger. I have included it here for easy reference and comparison to the multiple trigger combinations. Each trigger description includes a summary table and concentration chart. The summary table highlights the supplements used, the effective dose range (including the dose I typically use), and the best time to take the supplements.

The concentration curves give a visual representation of how the supplements work together on a time basis and show the window of opportunity for experiencing a lucid dream. The concentration curve for the primary trigger shows that Choline plays a significant role in the first hour and then drops off quickly. It works synergistically with Galantamine to quickly build up ACh levels that improve your odds of becoming lucid.

The Primary Trigger Combination			
Supplements	Dose range	Author's dose	Time To Take
Galantamine	4-8 mg	8 mg	Taken together after 4 - 5 hours of sleep
Choline (Bitartrate or Citrate)	250 - 750 mg	500 mg	

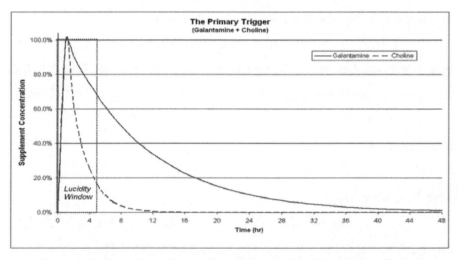

Concentration Curve for the Primary Trigger Combination (Galantamine + Choline)

The Extended Play Trigger:

This combination adds GPC to the primary trigger. Since GPC efficiently crosses the blood brain barrier and takes three hours to reach peak plasma levels, it picks up where Choline leaves off: Acetylcholine concentrations rise to a higher level and stay elevated for a longer period of time. This can result in extremely long lucid dreams. Two hours or more is not uncommon. Furthermore, this combination is very well tolerated at the effective dose level and I have never experienced negative side effects when using it. You can expect a strong transition and possibly hearing music during the course of the dream. If the music is too loud, reduce the dose of the GPC for the next attempt.

The Extended Play Trigger			
Supplements	Dose range	Author's dose	Time To Take
Galantamine	4-8 mg	8 mg	Taken together after 4 - 5 hours of sleep
Choline (Bitartrate or Citrate)	250 - 750 mg	500 mg	
GPC	300 - 900 mg	600 mg	

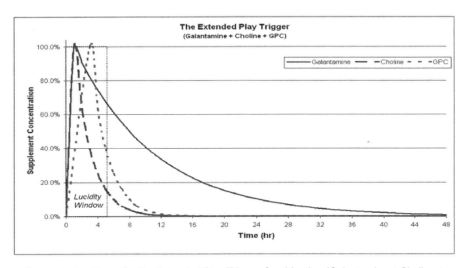

Concentration Curve for the Extended Play Trigger Combination (Galantamine + Choline + GPC)

The Soundtrack Trigger:

This combination adds Nicotine (via a patch) to the primary trigger. Although Nicotine has a number of negative characteristics, when combined with Galantamine it can produce phenomenal lucid dreams. Extremely strong transitions are possible and expect a vivid memory of the dream. Some of my favorite lucid dreams developed from this combination. In addition to visual and tactile vividness, these dreams can be characterized as having a heightened auditory sense. On many occasions I have experienced a soundtrack to my dreams that can be described as wonderful and original. To some degree, I have also experienced this phenomena using GPC, but with Nicotine the music seems to better match my mood and the dream plot. Negative side effects can be avoided if a low dose patch is placed on after four or five hours of sleep and immediately removed upon awakening. Due to the short term desensitization that Nicotine causes however, I typically take a full seven days off from supplements after using this combination.

The Soundtrack Trigger			
Supplements	Dose range	Author's dose	Time To Take
Galantamine	4-8 mg	8 mg	Taken together after 4 - 5 hours of sleep
Choline (Bitartrate or Citrate)	250 - 750 mg	500 mg	
Nicotine (patch)	7 mg or less	7 mg	Applied after 4-5 hours of sleep and removed immediately upon awakening

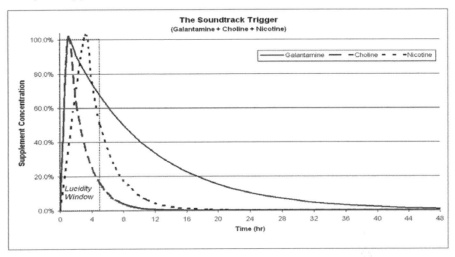

Concentration Curve for the Soundtrack Trigger Combination (Galantamine + Choline + Nicotine)

The Power of Reason Trigger:

This combination adds Yohimbine to the primary trigger. When Yohimbine is used correctly it can produce extremely high level lucid dreams. Where some of the other combinations may increase dream length, Yohimbine can increase the ability to think while within a dream. Advanced lucid dreaming involves more than just having a lucid dream; it involves moving through the dream with a clear mind so that you can consciously go deeper into the experience. Extremely small doses are all that are required; in fact, small doses are the optimum. The right dose will be one that does not significantly increase the time it takes to fall to sleep. Too large of dose will extend the time it takes to fall to sleep beyond the optimum time of the other supplements. This combination can cause extremely strong transitions.

The Power of Reason Trigger			
Supplements	Dose range	Author's dose	Time To Take
Galantamine	4-8 mg	8 mg	Taken together after 4 - 5 hours of sleep
Choline (Bitartrate or Citrate)	250 - 750 mg	500 mg	
Yohimbine	0.25 - 0.75 mg	0.35 mg	

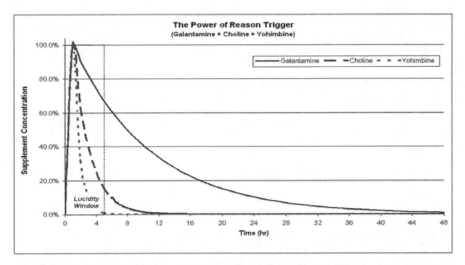

Concentration Curve for the Power of Reason Trigger Combination (Galantamine + Choline + Yohimbine)

The Trifecta Trigger:

This combination adds both GPC and Yohimbine to the primary trigger. It is the only triple trigger combination I have included. Transitions are intense so be prepared. As is true for any combination that leads to long lucid experiences, you may want to consciously bring yourself out of the dream from time to time and then go back in. This will help to remember more of the details of the entire dream.

The Trifecta Trigger			
Supplements	Dose range	Author's dose	Time To Take
Galantamine	4-8 mg	8 mg	Taken together after 4 - 5 hours of sleep
Choline (Bitartrate or Citrate)	250 - 750 mg	500 mg	
GPC	300 - 900 mg	600 mg	
Yohimbine	0.25 - 0.75 mg	0.35 mg	

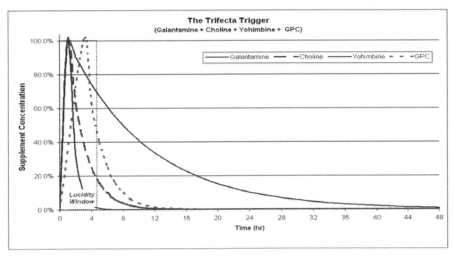

Concentration Curve for the Trifecta Trigger Combination
(Galantamine+Choline+Yohimbine+GPC)

How to use the Multiple Trigger Combinations:

The procedure outlined on page 127 gives a good outline of basic steps used to induce lucid dreams. "Part 4 - Improving Your Odds" goes into the more detail and includes many useful tips and techniques. If you are not using Piracetam immediately following your attempts, you should take at least four nights off between tries. You may find your need five, six, or even seven nights off in order to get consistent results. If you use Nicotine, I recommend you wait a full seven days before making another attempt. If you use Piracetam, remember that it is very important to take the first dose immediately after awakening from an attempt. When using Piracetam, you should take at least one night off between attempts and you may find that two or even three nights off are required for consistent results.

20

Supporting Supplements

This chapter summarizes how to use Mucuna Pruriens, Piracetam, 5-HTP, and Melatonin to support and enhance lucid dreaming.

Increasing Dream Control: Mucuna Pruriens

When used correctly, Mucuna Pruriens can have a strong effect on lucid dreams. It does so by increasing dopamine levels in the brain which leads to a state of increased confidence, motivation, and an almost total lack of fear from within the dream state. With this emotional boost, practically anything is possible. Previously, I mentioned the positive effects Mucuna Pruriens has on flying and changing the dreamscape, but its effects go further than that. I have walked into a raging fire and absorbed the energy of the flames, created a thunderstorm and guided lightning bolts into my hands, stood on the tracks as a speeding train passed right through me, and climbed a mountain to the summit, then just casually stepped off the edge, and much more. Mucuna Pruriens can create a true adventure in your lucid dreams. That being said, Mucuna can be a little tricky to use. Large doses of Mucuna (100 mg or more of L-dopa) taken with a trigger will reduce your odds of becoming lucid (although you will most likely experience extremely vivid dreams).

Smaller doses will give you an edge but may not have as big as impact on control as the larger doses do. One proven solution is to take Mucuna an hour or so prior to taking the trigger.

Mucuna Pruriens can be added to any of the trigger combinations listed previously. If you are going to take the Mucuna simultaneously with the trigger you should take a dose that contains less than 100 mg of L-dopa (see chapter 11). If you want to try a larger dose (100-200 mg L-dopa), you should take it an hour or so before taking the trigger. You can either sleep or stay awake for the hour between doses. The following tables show the two methods of combining Mucuna Pruriens with the primary trigger combination.

The Primary Trigger Combination PLUS Mucuna Pruriens (A)			
Supplements	Dose range	Author's dose	Time To Take
Galantamine	4-8 mg	8 mg	Taken together after 4 - 5 hours of sleep
Choline (Bitartrate or Citrate)	250 - 750 mg	500 mg	
Mucuna Pruriens	< 100 mg L-dopa	80 mg L-dopa	

The Primary Trigger Combination PLUS Mucuna Pruriens (B)			
Supplements	Dose range	Author's dose	Time To Take
Mucuna Pruriens	<200 mg L-dopa content	160 mg L-dopa	Taken after 4 hours of sleep
Galantamine	4-8 mg	8 mg	Taken together ~1 hour after taking Mucuna Pruriens
Choline (Bitartrate or Citrate)	250 - 750 mg	500 mg	

Counteracting Desensitization and Tolerance: Piracetam

Piracetam can increase the frequency you can take supplements and succeed in having a lucid dream. Without Piracetam, one or two nights per week are about the limit. With Piracetam, three or four nights per week are possible. Even with Piracetam however, you may have to take a few extra days off from every so often. It's best to keep your dream schedule flexible. For example, I might have three or four nights of lucid dreaming in one particular week. If I notice that my transitions are becoming weaker as the days go by, I know that I am approaching a dry spell. In order to get back to where I started I will generally take a few extra nights off before making another attempt. You will need to use your own judgment as to what works best for you.

The details of using Piracetam were described earlier (See chapter 18), but remember that for Piracetam to be most effective, you should take a dose immediately after waking up from each attempt. This allows Piracetam to counter ACh levels when they are at their highest and therefore keeps desensitization to a minimum.

Improving Quality of Sleep: 5-HTP

5-HTP can be used as a means of suppressing REM sleep in the first half of the night. This allows you to have longer natural REM periods during the time that you are attempting a lucid dream. It also helps balance your sleep. This is especially important if you are attempting to have multiple nights per week of supplement induced lucid dreaming. The triggers can often leave you feeling fatigued the next day, even when they are taken after 4 or 5 hours of sleep. When the triggers are preceded by 5-HTP, your overall sleep is of a higher quality and you feel much more refreshed upon awakening.

The following table and concentration chart show how 5-HTP is used in accordance with the primary trigger combination. The optimum dose of 5-HTP will be the one that results in the most vivid dreams after four or five hours of sleep. 5-HTP can precede any of the trigger combinations.

The Primary Trigger Combination PLUS Mucuna Pruriens (B)			
Supplements	Dose range	Author's dose	Time To Take
5-HTP	100 - 150 mg	100 mg	Taken at bedtime
Galantamine	4-8 mg	8 mg	Taken together after 4 - 5 hours of
Choline (Bitartrate or Citrate)	250 - 750 mg	500 mg	sleep

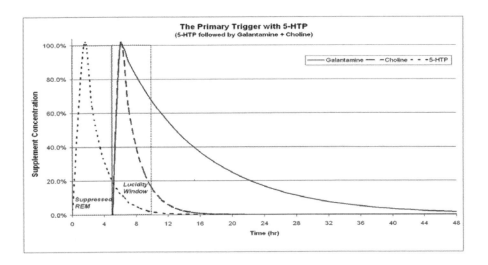

Counteracting Insomnia: Melatonin

If you find that you have trouble falling back to sleep after taking any one of the trigger combinations, you may consider adding a little Melatonin to the mix. The testing I did showed that a small of dose of Melatonin (<0.5 mg) could cut the time to fall back to sleep in half and still maintain high odds of having a successful lucid dream. Larger doses help me fall to sleep faster, but generally reduced my odds of success. The ideal time to fall to sleep after taking the trigger supplements is 40 – 60 minutes. This is the time that most of the triggers are reaching their maximum plasma levels and tends to be the time the strongest transitions occur. If you find you are staying awake much longer than this during an attempt, then Melatonin may actually increase your odds of success by letting you fall to sleep closer to the optimum time. The following table shows how Melatonin can be used in accordance with the primary trigger combination.

The Primary Trigger Combination PLUS Melatonin			
Supplements	Dose range	Author's dose	Time To Take
Galantamine	4-8 mg	8 mg	Taken together after 4 - 5 hours of sleep
Choline (Bitartrate or Citrate)	250 - 750 mg	500 mg	
Melatonin	0.3 - 0.5 mg	0.33 mg	

__Part 4:__

Improving Your Odds

Now I will discuss several strategies that you can use to greatly improve your odds of becoming lucid, lengthen the time spent in the lucid state, and increase the control you have over the dream. Some of these practices have been known to lucid dreamers for over a generation, others were adapted from my qigong practice, and a few were developed by more or less hit and miss experimentation tactics during my own lucid dream development.

21

Daytime Practice

The first fact the lucid dreamer is forced to accept is that the dream world is every bit as detailed and real as the physical world. Once this is realized, one soon comes to realize the second fact; the physical world is every bit as subjective and insubstantial as the dream world. These two realizations can not be fully intellectualized and must be experienced first hand in order to grasp the profound nature of lucid dreaming and also of being physically awake.

In my lucid dream experiences I have found there are two primary types of dream characters: the ignorant and the alive. The ignorant characters are more or less mindless, just playing out their role in the dream and having no ability to actually think. Their ignorance becomes fully apparent when you, in a fully lucid state, attempt to have a conversation with them. Ask them a question that requires thought or self-reflection and they are dumbfounded. Even the simplest questions like, "What are you thinking about?", "Tell me about yourself.", or "What is your name?" will yield a mindless and empty response.

There is however a totally different type of character. They tend to be fully animated and can express their own opinions that may be remarkably different from your own. They have the ability to adapt and to think on their feet and can sometimes even outsmart you in a game of wits.

When we are in a dream but are not lucid, we resemble the first type of character, the ignorant. We're unaware of what we're doing; we just do it. We don't think; we don't recognize the things we should; we are just acting out a part in a play we know nothing about. When we are present in the dream in full lucidity on the other hand, we resemble the second type of character. We are alive and know the situation. We can lead and take control of the situation. We have transformed ourselves from pure determinists, who take no real responsibility, into examples of freewill by actively guiding the situation and therefore our lives.

After this is fully experienced and realized in the dream state one may start to notice a similar characterization in the physical state. Consider the times we follow through with our daily activities in a mechanical manner, blindly going about some activity for whatever reason. Remember that the goal is to become lucid, not just in the dream state but also in the physical state and also remember that maintaining lucidity in one state helps in achieving lucidity in the other state. One should strive to be alive and lucid in every instant in the physical as well as in the dream.

Often when I first enter a lucid dream I notice that although I am walking about, my vision is quite hazy and blurred. I have learned that by paying very close attention to the details surrounding me and by looking into things instead of just looking at them, my vision suddenly snaps into clear and vivid focus. The same principle can be applied during waking life. Lucidity is not a special type of dream phenomena; it is a special type of life phenomena.

In addition to constantly striving for lucidity one should constantly be considering whether they are currently in the dream state or the physical state. It is not a given that you are awake and in the physical state at any given moment. The dream world can be every bit as mundane as the physical and the physical world can be every bit as exciting as the dream. Both worlds can come with exquisite detail and beauty or perhaps blandness and ugliness. The true lucid dreamer knows that the two worlds can not be easily distinguished with just a glance or passing thought. You may think you are definitely awake, but let me assure you that there are many times that you are absolutely positive you awake but instead are fully engaged in a dream. Simple tests can be done to help you distinguish the difference and you should get in to the habit of carrying out these tests on a frequent basis.

It is a false assumption that the dream world has no rules. In fact, not only do rules exist but the two worlds have much in common. For example, there are no new colors in the dream world; in fact there are no new sensations of any kind in the dream world. Gravity does exist in the dream world; it is just that you have the ability to manipulate it. Pain can exist in the dream world as well; both emotional and physical. Solid substances exist in the dream world; it is just that you have the ability to transcend them. The only two significant differences are that:

1. It is easier to manipulate your surroundings in the dream world.
2. For most of us the physical world is more based on repeating cycles than the dream world. Yesterday may not be that different from today (I got up, took a shower, drove to work, ate lunch, drove home, played with the kids, ate dinner, then

went to bed). The dream world however, seems to be more or less free from cycles. Every experience is a new and different set of circumstances.

It is wise to keep these things in mind as you move through the physical and into the dream and then back to the physical. Continually test your state. Does this place look familiar? Am I supposed to be here? What was I doing ten minutes ago? If there is any hint that something isn't quite as you would expect, try hovering off the ground a little bit, or changing the color of the grass, or walking through a wall, or anything else until you are absolutely convinced that you know which state you are in: the physical or the dream. Continual practice of this will spill over into the dream and is remarkably effective at waking you up within the dream.

The real first step in advanced lucid dreaming is to set your intention to become fully lucid in both states and to continually prove to yourself which state you in at any given time.

22

Preparation and Transitioning

If you choose to try some of the techniques I presented in this book you will undoubtedly find there are some very subtle factors that ultimately determine whether or not you are successful. This chapter summarizes what I have learned through countless lucid dream attempts (both successful and unsuccessful) as to what has the biggest impact of actually "making it in" and achieving a successful WILD.

1. Create a peaceful environment.

    Sleep time should be peaceful and free of distractions. When you are on the edge that separates wakefulness from the lucid dream the last thing you need is to have something from the external world grab your attention. Noise can be big factor. At four in the morning the quietest sound can capture your mind and become an annoying nuisance. You may want to wear earplugs when attempting to have a lucid dream or perhaps even a mask over your eyes. The more you can isolate yourself from your external senses the better your chances of quickly entering the dream.

2. Don't sacrifice your quality of sleep.

    I have seen it happen. People can get too carried away with lucid dreaming; obsessed with it. It's new, it's cool, and it may hold the key to many secrets locked away within the subconscious, but it is not worth sacrificing your health.

Without good health, you have nothing. Poor sleep usually carries with it a number of ramifications. You may not be the best husband or wife that you could, or the best father or mother, or the best employee, or the best anything. It may take a toll on your happiness, peace of mind, and on the strength of your immune system. Don't go down that path. It is possible to have frequent high level lucid dreams and still maintain a balanced sleep schedule. I firmly believe everyone should take at least one night off between lucid dream attempts. Not only does this allow you to fully digest your last lucid dream and properly prepare for the next one, but by taking a night off you allow your body catch up on whatever sleep it needs.

3. Waking up just the right amount.

       In my own practice, I have focused on developing the ability to consistently achieve WILDs. The triggers described in this book also increase the odds of achieving DILDs and depending on whether you are going for a WILD or a DILD will influence what you do just after you take the supplements. If you favor DILDs, your goal will be to avoid insomnia by falling back to sleep soon after taking the supplements. You should wake up, go to the toilet, take the supplements, lie back down, and relax. The less time you're up, the better the odds of falling quickly back to sleep. Avoid turning on bright lights. Avoid climbing up or down stairs and any other activity that might increase your heart rate. Some of these supplements start to work fast and the longer you're awake, the more difficult it will be to fall back to sleep. Purposely avoid becoming too alert and learn to stay in a relaxed state. These are the keys to quickly getting back to sleep.

WILDs require a different approach. You should neither wake up too much nor fall to sleep too early. Fall to sleep too early and the supplements won't be working adequately to assist you with the transition. Wake up too much and you could end up lying in bed for hours with insomnia. Falling to sleep 40 – 60 minutes after taking the supplements is ideal. It is within this time frame I find the transitions to be the most vibrant and the duration of lucid dreams to be the longest. My approach is to wake up, go to the toilet, take the supplements and lie back down. Just as in the case of the DILD, I try to not to become too alert and hope to maintain a feeling of drowsiness. I stay relaxed, but instead of hoping to fall quickly back to sleep, I gently remind myself of what my dream goals are. Just prior to nodding off, I slightly open my eyes just enough to let some ambient light enter my field of vision. The opening of my eyes is so slight that an observer would likely not notice it at all. I then relax and let my eyes naturally close and relax. I repeat this once or twice more. Each time I get close to losing consciousness I crack open my eyes for only an instant. By this time five to ten minutes have passed since taking the supplements. I then casually and sleepily practice an exercise I call "arms and legs qigong" followed by "seeded" visualizations. Both of these exercises are described below. During these exercises I continue to crack my eyes open any time I feel I am about to fall to sleep. With this approach I can stay right on the border that separates wakefulness from sleep until a transition occurs.

4. Quieting the mind.

The biggest influence that keeps you from falling back to sleep after you have taken a supplement is that annoying little voice in your head that just won't seem to shut up. Right after you lie back down it is a good idea to spend five or ten minutes going over what it is that you want to accomplish in the dream, but after that you need to turn off the voice. This can be a bit tricky. You might find yourself wondering what time it is, or wondering if the supplements are starting to work, or complaining about your body position, or whatever. The fact is that the longer you talk to yourself, the longer you are going to stay awake. Since your mind is awake it wants to be active, and thinking in words seems to be its first choice of activity. You will need to learn how to quiet the mind. The easiest way is to let your mind get caught up in some other, non-verbal activity like tactile or visual exercises. But even then the voice will come through again and again and try to win over your attention. Ignore it and let it go. The biggest mistake you can make is to get frustrated. Calmness and patience are words to live by in this situation. Simply go back to the tactile or visual exercise that you were doing and don't give it another thought.

5. Loosing the body (Arms and legs qigong).

An excellent way to quiet the mind and prepare for the transition from the physical state to the lucid dream state is to do tactile exercise. Tactile exercises are ones that involve imagining the sensation of motion. They are analogous to visualizations except that they make use of the sense of touch instead of the sense of sight. Remember that about 90% of my lucid dreams using supplements involve me getting up and walking away from my physical body fully integrated within a dream body. By using tactile exercises, you are preparing the mind for this type of transition. I have tried many types of tactile exercises: walking, running, climbing, spinning, floating, etc; but the ones that work best for me are the ones in which I imagine part of my dream body slipping out of my physical body and then slipping back in and then repeating this over and over again. My favorite of these exercises is one in which I imagine either my arms or legs (or both) floating downward on each exhale and then rising up on each inhale. For example, as I exhale a breath, I feel my legs bend at the knee forcing my imaginary feet and calves to rotate downward and leave my physical body. By the end of the exhale my imaginary knee has rotated a full ninety degrees such that my imaginary feet are dangling below my body. On the inhale, I rotate my imaginary knee in the opposite direction in order to raise my imaginary legs back up. By the end of the inhale I have brought my imaginary legs all the way up and even slightly through my physical legs so that they are suspended above my body. I keep repeating this over and over again as I lie there. Another variant is to visualize my arms bending at the shoulder in a similar manner or to do both my arms and legs together. I usually lie on my back while doing this exercise and do it for about 10-20 minutes. After that I roll over onto my right side and do "seeded" visualization exercises until the dream starts.

6. Initiating (but not forcing) visualization (Seeded visualizations)

At this point I am very close to sleep and the supplements are starting to work. Now it's time to try to get the dream started. Active visualization does not work for me because the focus it takes to actively visualize something ends up keeping me awake. Purely passive visualization doesn't work very well either, because sometimes the images don't come and I end up hearing my thoughts instead. What works best is what I call seeded visualizations. A seeded visualization is one that I actively start but then immediately let go and passively let it develop on its own. Instead of actively trying to keep a visualization going, I just keep on dropping seeds until they take off on their own. This technique is very effective. I might visualize a place, an object, or a person just long enough to really see the image and then I let go. If nothing happens after a little while, I do it again and again and so on. These flashes of visualization tend to make other flashes start to happen that gradually get longer in duration. It gets to the point that I drop a seed and end up almost entering a dream but then come out. Then I seed another one and almost enter a dream but then come out. Then I seed another one and before you know it I am caught up in a transition from the physical state into the lucid dream state.

7. Patience

The method that I have described definitely requires patience. Always remain calm and relaxed. Don't allow yourself to get anxious even if you have been lying awake far too long. Just relax. The dreams will come. As soon as your patience wears thin, you will undoubtedly start talking to yourself and complaining. This will further reduce your chances of success. Just lie there and relax and the dreams will come.

8. Transitioning

Transitioning refers to the experience of moving from the physical state into the dream state with a continuous, unbroken thread of consciousness. When you experience a transition, you do not lose your identity; nor do you lose your memory; nor do you lose train of thought: not even for a split second. It is a continuum of consciousness. Transitioning from the physical state into the dream state is one of the most profound experiences someone can achieve. The methods in this book lead to WILDs. Wake induced lucid dreams include a conscious transition from the physical state into the dream state. This type of transition is what the Tibetan dream yogis strive for. It is often referred to as an out of body experience, an astral journey or perhaps a spirit quest. Although the experience of this type of transition is identical for all of these systems, the belief structures that support it can be very different from one another. Lucid dreamers believe it is a transition into a dream. Once inside the dream you can better tap into the subconscious that may hold many yet to be discovered secrets. The Tibetans believe that the transition is a rehearsal for death so that one can learn to maintain awareness after the physical life ceases with the hope of breaking the endless cycle of reincarnation. The out of body believers perceive it to be one body leaving another; the astral body being of a finer type of energy which has the ability to walk the physical earth or enter the astral planes. The spirit quest practitioners believe it to be a journey for knowledge or healing purposes, one in which you may encounter ancient ancestors or great teachers that possess metaphysic abilities. Maybe one of them right, maybe none of them are right, or maybe all of them are right. I do know that the experience will change your life forever and that it is at the fingertips of everybody who follows the methods in this book.

Although the experience can never be fully intellectualized, I have learned a few tricks of the trade that may assist you. This section summarizes the method that consistently works for me.

i.   Learn to recognize when a transition is about to occur:

There are several signs you will recognize as you get more practice. The first sign is that dream imagery gets stronger and lengthier. When you are continually seeding your visualization, there comes a point where they start to take off. You are almost drawn into the dream but then you come out, then almost in again, and then out. The second sign is that you may experience intense vibrations or a sensation of sudden acceleration. Both of these experiences can be overwhelming, especially if you're a novice. They can last for a minute or more which may seem like an eternity. My advice is to simply enjoy the ride. Don't try to move. Don't get scared or panicky. Just lie there and try to relax.

ii.   Relax:

If you are new to the sensations of transitioning, the idea of being able to relax may seem a little comical or, at the very least, impractical. However if you get too tense, or start to panic, or try to move, the sensations will just suddenly stop and you will be lying in your bed upset that you missed a great opportunity. Hence you really need to learn to relax during the experience. Here are a few guidelines that might help:

- Don't start taking to yourself. Saying things like, "Oh my God", or "Holy $*&@", or even "Stay calm", isn't going to help you make it into the dream state.
- Your breathing should be smooth and steady, but try not to focus on it. Just do a causal and passing check to make sure your breathing is calm.
- Focus on the sensations and soak in the experience. To put it another way: Enjoy it.

iii.   Feel the natural sensation first:

As the experience is ending you may feel like parts of your body are floating. It is very common for me to feel as if my legs are starting to float upwards towards the ceiling. Sometimes I also feel as though my entire body is starting to roll over or perhaps one arm is slowly rising. The feeling is very authentic. The floating is gentle as though gravity has just stopped affecting part of the body. The part of the body that is doing the floating also feels totally authentic. If your legs feel as though they are rising toward the ceiling, it is not as though an imaginary set of legs is rising while the physical legs lie on the bed. There are not two sets of legs in this experience, only one set exist and that is the set doing the floating. As far as your experience is concerned, your physical legs no longer exist.

iv.   Lead the natural sensation away:

The initial floating feeling occurs naturally. It is not as though you tried to imagine it. It just happens. Don't bring your attention back to physical body. For example, if you feel your legs floating up, don't bring your attention down to the bed where your legs are "supposed" to be in an effort to see whether or not your "real" legs are floating. Doing this will most likely end the experience and you would have missed a great opportunity. Instead lead your legs further away in the same direction that they feel like they're going. Here is where the arms and legs qigong exercise pays off. While you were practicing this you "felt" your legs floating down on the exhale and then guided them back up on the inhale. Now in the exact same manner as in that exercise, keep guiding your floating legs further and further in the same direction they are floating in. Since the legs are naturally attached to the rest of the body, as they move further away they end up carrying the rest of your body with them (where at this point your body is your dream body). It is really that easy. For example, my legs start to float up naturally and I then I carry them upward so my entire body is pulled upward following them. Then I guide them down to the floor so that I end up standing in the middle of the room. Another example, I feel my body naturally start to roll and I carry the motion forward so that I roll away from where I was sleeping and then stand up in the middle of the room.

v.   Keep going:

Once you're out, keep going. The transition is usually mostly or purely tactile. This means you feel it but you don't see or hear it. Once you get out, your sense of touch is vivid and alive but your other senses need to be cleaned up a bit before you can do much. Since your sense of touch is all you are relying on at his point, it is a good idea to keep it going by starting to walk forward. As you do so you may notice your vision starting to evolve. Mine is usually very hazy and blurry at this point. There are two exercises I do that have been very successful in snapping my vision into vivid focus. The first exercise is to look very closely at objects and try to see the small details. Keep moving but keep looking at things and notice the tiny features in them. The other exercise is to just jump up and down a bit while you are looking at whatever is in front of you. This keeps you moving but not moving forward so that the same object stays in front of you until it finally snaps into focus. It usually takes about 10 to 20 jumps before my sight is clear and vivid. At this point you may notice that you are standing in your bedroom and can walk about your house at your leisure. The detail is incredible and can be totally convincing that you really are walking around your physical house. I tend to believe it is a dream duplicate of the house. But I will leave it for you to decide for yourself. I get bored walking around a dark house at 4 AM so I usually venture outside. Once outside I either consciously change my location or it happens spontaneously and the lucid dream goes on from there.

Another form of this type of exit, that is perhaps easier for the novice to successfully complete, involves rotating your body. Once you feel part of your body start to float in any direction, guide that part around in a large circular motion so your legs are pulled around to the headboard of the bed, continuing back the footboard, back to the headboard and so on. When done correctly, this will generate a totally authentic sensation of rotation. You don't need to turn fast, just keep the motion going for as long as you can. When you stop you will find that you are fully within the dream.

23

Breaking Down the Wall

There is a wall that divides the physical world from the dream world. This division is the fundamental feature that keeps us all from entering the lucid dream state readily and easily. The division is mysterious, daunting and historically has only been crossed by a few lucky or talented people. The information herein opens up this experience to practically anyone who is willing and able to try, and the experience allows us to ask, "What is it that creates this wall in the first place?" One popular answer is that this wall is created by a loss of consciousness; when we go to sleep we simply lose consciousness and the ego ceases to exist. I have serious doubts about this theory. In my view it is not consciousness that fails us, it is our memory. No memory results in a loss of identity but not lack of consciousness. Based on personal experience, I do not agree with either dream theory presented in the beginning of this book. I believe we are continually dreaming throughout the night. I believe our consciousness is always continuous during every instant of our existence. I believe it is our memory that breaks down during sleep leaving us with almost complete amnesia. It is no coincidence that the best lucid dream triggers are powerful memory boosters. Today's dream theories are based on the premise that when people are awakened from deep sleep, they don't <u>remember</u> their dreams.

Researchers extrapolate this to mean that they don't dream during deep sleep, as if the ability to remember and the ability to experience were the same thing. The Tibetans believe it is possible to hold on to consciousness during deep sleep and to actually remember it when you wake up. If we are to become the best that we can become with our lucid dream development, we must learn how to break down this wall. I have developed an exercise that is designed to do just that.

Most people rarely remember their dreams. Night after night we enter a dream world filled with adventure and mystery, yet morning after morning we have absolutely no recollection of it. Most lucid dream enthusiasts keep a dream journal to try to break down this wall. Trying to remember your dreams does help and I do keep an active and up to date dream journal. There is another exercise however, that is at least ten times as beneficial. The wall that divides the dream from the physical is two sided and just as it is difficult to remember your dreams in the physical; it is equally difficult to remember the physical in your dreams.

At the beginning of every lucid dream I practice a few minutes of "physical recall". I have found that, when using the supplement approach to lucid dreaming, factual kinds of information are easy to recall, much easier than when no supplements are used. This is probably because both acetylcholine and norepinephrine boost memory and the best lucid dream triggers either boost acetylcholine or norepinephrine levels within the brain. Information like my name, address, family members' names and birthdays, even my credit card number are easily shouted out. The challenge comes when dealing with experiential memories. Trying to remember anything that I did that day is much more difficult. Ask yourself what you had for breakfast and you may find yourself standing there in the dream with your mouth hanging open saying "uhhhhhhhh". This ability can be drastically improved with practice, and as it improves you will find yourself having more and more high level lucid dreams, even on nights when no supplements are used. The approach I use is to think about a specific event that I want to remember as I am getting ready to enter a lucid dream. I purposely don't try to remember or rehearse all of the details; I just try to place the event firmly in my mind. Then when I get to the point that I am seeding my visualization, I do so by giving myself short visual snapshots of different parts of the memory. After I enter the lucid state I keep seeding the dream with the same kind of visual snapshots. This transforms the dream into a reenactment of the memory. It is an amazing experience. If left unattended the dream will naturally go off on some tangent but if you keep dropping the seeds it can snap the dream back to acting out the memory. This undeniably leads to the best recall of any event because you actually relive it instead of just remember it. Doing this exercise on a regular basis actively breaks down the wall that separates the two states. You will find that you are remembering dreams in great detail even on the nights that you don't use supplements and you will find that you can start to recall more and more of the details from your physical life while in the dream. When you really start to remember your physical life while in dream, you naturally start to have lucid dreams much more often. It becomes easy to recognize the dream state. This exercise also has a significant impact on dream recall. Understand that vivid sensory experience and vivid recall are not synonymous. Performing this exercise while you are also actively trying to remember your dreams when you awake, acts to break down the wall from both sides and once the wall starts to fall, lucidity goes way up.

24

Keeping an Up to Date Log

Beyond just keeping a dream journal, you should keep an up to date log that documents the details of each attempt you make at becoming lucid. After just a dozen or so high level lucid dreams, you can gain a great many insights by going over the details of each trial. The log will highlight statistical trends and show you what combinations work the best and how the various combinations affect the lucid dream. I recommend that you include the following information:

- Date
- The supplements that you took
- The dose of each supplement
- The time that you took the supplements
- How many hours of sleep you had before you took each supplement
- Whether or not you were dreaming when you woke up to take the supplements
- Any other important notes about the supplements
- What exercises you did when you first lay down after taking the supplements
- How long it took to fall to back to sleep or enter the lucid dream
- What your sleep position was.
- Details about the transition into the dream

- Did your feel accelerations, vibrations, or floatiness. If so rank the intensity
- Rank the resulting dream quality
- Rank your ability to recall the dream
- Rank your visual vividness
- Rank your tactile vividness
- Rank your auditory vividness
- Rank your participation level (i.e. did you just observe the dream or were you actively involved)
- Rank your lucidity level
- Was it a DILD or a WILD
- Rank your ability to control your reasoning within the dream.
- Rank your ability to control your emotions within the dream.
- Rank your ability to control your will within the dream
- Note if there were any physical side effects
- Note if there were any mental side effects
- Note if there were any emotional side effects (crying, laughing, etc)
- List some general notes about the experience
- Summarize the dream
- List any lessons learned or theories that came out of the dream.

Although the list may seem extensive, it only takes about ten to twenty minutes to fill out if you set up a simple spreadsheet. This is a great way to archive your development that goes far beyond just keeping a dream journal.

25

Where Do I go From Here?

Hopefully this book will open up the world of high level lucid dreaming to a much wider audience. But now that you can have high level lucid dreams, then what? Is a dream just a dream or is there more to it than that? Can we uncover and tap into our own hidden potentials? Can we find answers concerning life, death, and why we're here? The potentials are enormous but the territory is almost entirely unmapped. Once high level lucid dreams become common place, then the real advancement will start to happen. Can we heal ourselves or others from within a dream? Can we purposefully enter another persons dream? Can we bring back knowledge from the dream state into the physical state? The next several decades should prove to be enormously exciting and rich with discovery. I look forward to being part of that experience and I hope you will to.

Please visit www.AdvancedLD.com and let me know how you are doing and feel free to ask any questions that you might have. Also watch the website for new discoveries concerning the supplement approach and I invite you join some of the research studies sponsored on the site. If you need help locating any of the supplements referred to in this book, visit www.AdvancedLD.com\links.html and find links to all of the distributors that I regularly use plus ones that have been recommended to me.

If you enjoyed this book, watch for upcoming publications that will focus on advanced lucid dreaming techniques and applications. Also feel free to email me with questions and comments.

Good Luck to All!

Thomas Yuschak

tyuschak@AdvancedLD.com

References

1. Theoretical Background References

    a. Sleep Cycle

        i. http://www.sleepdisorderchannel.com/stages/

        ii. http://en.wikipedia.org/wiki/Sleep#Sleep_physiology

    b. REM Rebound

    c. Dream Theories

        i. http://www.psychoanalysis.org.uk/solms4.htm

        ii. http://psych.ucsc.edu/dreams/Library/domhoff_2001a.html

        iii. http://www.bbsonline.org/Preprints/OldArchive/bbs.solms.html

        iv. http://serendip.brynmawr.edu/bb/neuro/neuro01/web1/MillerJ.html

    d. Neurotransmitters

        i. http://web.umr.edu/~rhall/neuroscience/03_sleep/sleepneuro.pdf

        ii. http://www.ifisiol.unam.mx/Brain/trnsmt.htm

        iii. http://www.benbest.com/science/anatmind/anatmd10.html

        iv. http://bipolar.about.com/cs/neurotrans/l/aa0007_msngrs.htm

     v.   http://thedea.org/yourbrain.html

    vi.   http://www.neurosci.pharm.utoledo.edu/MBC3 320/nicotinic.htm

   vii.   http://www.raysahelian.com/dopamine.html

2.   Individual Supplement References

    a.   Galantamine

         i.   http://www.galantamine.cc/research/galantami ne-research-38.htm

        ii.   http://www.galantamine.cc/galantamine-12.htm

       iii.   http://www.galantamine.cc/galantamine-6.htm

       iv.   http://www.galantamine.cc/galantamine-11.htm

        v.   http://www.galantamine.cc/research/galantami ne-research-27.htm

       vi.   http://www.galantamine.cc/research/galantami ne-research-11.htm

      vii.   http://www.galantamine.cc/galantamine-17.htm

     viii.   http://www.galantamine.cc/galantamine-24.htm

      ix.   http://www.galantamine.cc/galantamine-10.htm

       x.   http://www.birf.info/home/bi-tools/qlinks_memo.html#Galantamine

      xi.   http://www.galantamine.cc/galantamine-9.htm

    b.   GPC (Glycerophosphocholine)

         i.   http://www.dockidd.com/pdf2/GPCMindBody,4 _14_05.pdf

        ii.   http://www.dockidd.com/pdf2/GPCasInjectable, 4_14_05.pdf

       iii.   http://www.pdrhealth.com/drug_info/nmdrugpro files/nutsupdrugs/lal_0153.shtml

        iv.   http://www.lef.org/magazine/mag2003/jul2003_abs_03.html

  c. Nicotine

        i.   http://www.medsafe.govt.nz/profs/Datasheet/n/Nicotrolpatch.htm

        ii.   http://www.quitworks.org/docs/PharmoGuide_small.pdf

        iii.   http://science.howstuffworks.com/nicotine4.htm

        iv.   http://www.as.uky.edu/Biology/faculty/cooper/Bio401G/nicotineDesen.pdf

        v.   http://cds.ismrm.org/ismrm-2001/PDF2/0538.pdf

        vi.   http://www.blackwell-synergy.com/doi/pdf/10.1046/j.1471-4159.1994.63020561.x

        vii.   http://jp.physoc.org/cgi/content/abstract/553/3/857

        viii.   http://www.drugs.com/Nicotine/index.html

        ix.   http://www.trdrp.org/research/PageGrant.asp?grant_id=1853

  d. Piracetam

        i.   http://www.bulknutrition.com/?ingredients_id=41

        ii.   http://www.bulknutrition.com/a87_Brain_Food__Piracetam_II.html

        iii.   http://www.ceri.com/noot.htm

        iv.   http://emc.medicines.org.uk/emc/assets/c/html/displaydoc.asp?documentid=16509

v. http://www.antiaging-systems.com/a2z/nootropics.htm

vi. http://www.ceri.com/pira97.htm

vii. http://www.lef.org/prod_hp/abstracts/piracetam.html

viii. http://www.piracetam.com/

ix. http://www.worldhealth.net/p/1010,2056.html

x. http://www.piracetam.com/piracetam-12.htm

xi. http://www.piracetam.com/piracetam-26.htm

xii. http://www.piracetam.com/piracetam-11.htm

e. Mucuna Pruriens & L-Dopa

i. http://www.parkinson.org/site/pp.asp?c=9dJFJLPwB&b=184301

ii. http://www.rain-tree.com/velvetbean.htm

iii. http://www.ncbi.nlm.nih.gov/entrez/query.fcgi?cmd=Retrieve&db=PubMed&list_uids=15478206&dopt=Abstract

iv. http://www.healthyeatingclub.com/APJCN/Volume2/vol2.2/kempster.htm

v. http://www.neuroskills.com/tbi/motor.shtml

vi. http://www.neurology.org/cgi/content/abstract/61/7/1008

vii. http://www.raysahelian.com/mucunapruriens.html

viii. http://www3.interscience.wiley.com/cgi-bin/abstract/109672614/ABSTRACT?CRETRY=1&SRETRY=0

    f.   Yohimbine

        i.   http://en.wikipedia.org/wiki/Norepinephrine

       ii.   http://www.biopsychiatry.com/yohimin.htm

     iii.   http://www.biopsychiatry.com/yohimbine.htm

     iv.   http://www.biopsychiatry.com/norad.htm

      v.   http://www.ncbi.nlm.nih.gov/entrez/query.fcgi?c
md=Retrieve&db=PubMed&list_uids=6100759
&dopt=Abstract

     vi.   http://www.raysahelian.com/yohimbe.html

   vii.   http://jcp.sagepub.com/cgi/content/abstract/34/
5/418

  viii.   http://www.general-
anaesthesia.com/alpha2.html

    g.   5-HTP (5-hydroxytryptophan)

        i.   http://www.raysahelian.com/5-htp.html

       ii.   http://www.healthyplace.com/communities/depr
ession/treatment/alternative/brain_chemistry_2
.asp

     iii.   http://www.biopsychiatry.com/5htp.html

     iv.   http://web.mit.edu/dick/www/pdf/989.pdf

      v.   http://www.life-
enhancement.com/article_template.asp?ID=31
4

     vi.   http://www.holistic-
online.com/remedies/Sleep/sleep_ins_melatoni
n-and-5HTP.htm

   vii.   http://www.1fast400.com/i60_5-HTP.html

h. Melatonin

   i. http://web.mit.edu/newsoffice/1999/melatonin-1103.html

   ii. http://www.holistic-online.com/remedies/Sleep/sleep_ins_melatonin-and-5HTP.htm

   iii. http://www.charm.net/~profpan/armitage.html

   iv. http://jcem.endojournals.org/cgi/content/abstract/89/1/128

   v. http://www.raysahelian.com/melatonin.html

3. Desensitization and tolerance

   a. http://cds.ismrm.org/ismrm-2001/PDF2/0538.pdf

   b. http://www.as.uky.edu/Biology/faculty/cooper/Bio401G/nicotineDesen.pdf

   c. http://www.blackwell-synergy.com/doi/pdf/10.1046/j.1471-4159.1994.63020561.x

   d. http://www.currentseparations.com/issues/15-2/cs15-2d.pdf

   e. http://jp.physoc.org/cgi/content/abstract/553/3/857

   f. http://www.trdrp.org/research/PageGrant.asp?grant_id=1853

   g. http://www.piracetam.com/piracetam-12.htm

4. Misc

   a. http://members.aol.com/atracyphd/syndrome.htm

   b. http://www.clevelandclinic.org/health/health-info/docs/0900/0929.asp?index=5580&src=news

-

Index

Index

Printed in Great Britain by
Amazon.co.uk, Ltd.,
Marston Gate.